W9-CFV-082
.540 00296 9531

j947.58 Spi
Spilling, Michael.
Georgia
31540002969531

OCT 20 2008

CULTURES OF THE WORLD

GEORGIA

Marshall Cavendish Benchmark
New York

DISCARD

PICTURE CREDITS
Cover photo: © Peter Turnley/Corbis
Alt.TYPE / Reuters: 3, 5, 16, 32, 46, 47, 57, 59, 76, 86, 90 • Axiom: 13, 41, 42, 61, 61, 69, 71, 77, 87, 95 • Bjorn Klingwall: 53, 63, 70 • Eye Ubiquitous / Hutchison: 8, 15 • Hulton Getty: 19, 23, 26, 28, 29, 30, 31, 66, 81 • Hutchison Library: 4, 7, 35, 48, 50, 64, 65, 75, 97, 101, 119, 124 • Lonely Planet Images: 1, 18, 34, 68, 73, 78, 92, 96, 108, 116, 123 • MCIA—Thomas Khoo: 130, 131 • Mikhail Idamkin: 106, 107 • National Geographic Image Collection: 10, 54, 55, 60, 88, 110, 112, 122 • Novosti: 24, 39, 72, 102, 103, 104, 105, 113, 117, 125, 126, 127 • Novosti (London): 11, 14, 20, 25, 40, 44, 52, 99, 100, 111, 128 • Parker Photo Agency: 121 • Photolibrary.com: 6, 22, 56, 58, 85 • Society for Cooperation in Russian and Soviet Studies: 89, 118 • Topham Picture Point / Novosti (London): 33, 38, 67, 79, 82, 84, 98, 109, 114

PRECEDING PAGE
The exterior of Odessa Hotel in Tbilisi.

Publisher (U.S.): Michelle Bisson
Editors: Deborah Grahame, Mabelle Yeo, Mindy Pang
Copyreader: Tara Koellhoffer
Cover picture researcher: Connie Gardner
Picture researcher: Thomas Khoo

Marshall Cavendish Benchmark
99 White Plains Road
Tarrytown, NY 10591
Web site: www.marshallcavendish.us

3 1540 00296 9531

© Times Media Private Limited 1997
© Marshall Cavendish International (Asia) Private Limited 2009
All rights reserved. First edition 2009.
® "Cultures of the World" is a registered trademark of Times Publishing Limited.

Originated and designed by Times Media Private Limited
An imprint of Marshall Cavendish International (Asia) Private Limited
A member of Times Publishing Limited

All rights reserved. No part of this publication may be reproduced, stored in a retrieval system or transmitted, in any form or by any means, electronic, mechanical, photocopying, recording or otherwise, without the prior permission of the copyright owner. Request for permission should be addressed to the Publisher.

Marshall Cavendish is a trademark of Times Publishing Limited.

All Internet sites were correct and accurate at the time of printing. All monetary figures in this publication are in U.S. dollars.

Library of Congress Cataloging-in-Publication Data
Spilling, Michael.
Georgia / by Michael Spilling & Winnie Wong. — Rev. 2nd ed.
p. cm. — (Cultures of the world)
Summary: "Provides comprehensive information on the geography, history, wildlife, governmental structure, economy, cultural diversity, religion, and culture of Georgia"—Provided by publisher.
Includes bibliographical references and index.
ISBN 978-0-7614-3033-9
1. Georgia (Republic)—Juvenile literature. 2. Georgia (Republic) I. Wong, Winnie. II. Title.
DK672.3.S68 2008
947.58—dc22 2007050796

Printed in China

7 6 5 4 3 2 1

CONTENTS

INTRODUCTION 5

GEOGRAPHY 7
From mountain peaks to swampy lowland • Regions • Cities • Climate • Flora and fauna

HISTORY 19
Early history • Colchis and Greece • The Iberians • Conversion to Christianity • Arab domination • David the Builder • Queen Tamar • The Mongol yoke • Ottoman Turkey and Safavid Persia • Russian annexation • Georgia under the tsars • Soviet Georgia • Recent history

GOVERNMENT 35
Recent events • The 1995 Constitution • Parliament • Political parties • Conflicts in Abkhazia and South Ossetia • Adjaria—Haven of stability • Relations with Russia

ECONOMY
From public to private ownership • Agriculture • Mineral wealth • Energy • Transportation • Tourism 47

ENVIRONMENT
Deforestation • Water pollution • Air pollution 55

GEORGIANS
Kartvelian peoples • Adjarians • Abkhazians • Ossetians • Other peoples • Dress 61

LIFESTYLE
Country and city life • High living • Hospitality • To your health! • Family and marriage • Male domination • Education • Work and welfare 69

Government building in the capital, Tbilisi.

RELIGION 79
Georgian Orthodox Church • Saint George • Church of the Life-Giving Pillar • Russian Orthodox Church • Armenian Apostolic Church • Islam • Judaism

LANGUAGE 87
Georgian • History of the Georgian language • The Georgian alphabet • Learning Georgian • Other tongues • Names • Publications, radio, and television • Communications

ARTS 97
Metalwork • Architecture • Literature • Painting • Music and ballet • Film

LEISURE 109
Song and dance • Mountain sports and pastimes • Other sports • Health resorts

FESTIVALS 117
Georgian Orthodox and folk holidays • Other religious festivals • Civil holidays

FOOD 123
The Georgian table • Drinks

MAP OF GEORGIA 132

ABOUT THE ECONOMY 135

ABOUT THE CULTURE 137

TIME LINE 138

GLOSSARY 140

FURTHER INFORMATION 141

BIBLIOGRAPHY 142

INDEX 143

In mountainous regions, the lifestyle is simpler and more traditional than in the lowland and urban areas.

INTRODUCTION

THE REPUBLIC OF GEORGIA is not to be confused with the American state of the same name. When we think of Georgia, two people come to mind—the renowned ballerina Nina Ananiashvili and the infamous dictator Joseph Stalin. Described variously as part of Europe, the Caucasus, or the Middle East, Georgia was a part of the Soviet Union until 1991. The Caucasus republic, called Sakartvelo (sa-KART-ve-lo) in the country's native tongue, is an ancient land with a painful yet triumphant history. The Greeks, Byzantines, Persians, Arabs, and Russians have all left their mark on Georgia. Consequently it is a land of many faiths, cultures, and languages. Despite these diverse influences the Georgians have tenaciously retained their unique traditions, orthodox religion, and ancient language. Independence brought with it many challenges, but the Georgians are determined to rebuild their country to create a better future.

GEOGRAPHY

SITUATED IN THE HEART of the Caucasus mountain range, on the eastern coast of the Black Sea, Georgia is separated from its giant northern neighbor, Russia, by 450 miles (723 km) of the main range of the Caucasus. To the east lies Azerbaijan (200 miles/322 km), to the south Turkey (157 miles/252 km), and to the southeast Armenia (102 miles/164 km). Surrounded by mountains and sea, the country is geographically self-contained, and this has helped it preserve its national identity and culture despite numerous foreign invasions.

Although 87 percent of Georgia is largely mountainous, the nation has a remarkably varied climate, ranging from warm subtropics on the Black Sea coast to cold winters in the ice-capped peaks of the Caucasus. This variety is even more noteworthy considering Georgia's relatively small size, which covers an area of 26,900 square miles (69,700 square km)—slightly smaller than South Carolina or about the same size as West Virginia.

Left: **Batumi waterfront facing the Black Sea.**

Opposite: **The beautiful snowcapped mountains of Bolshoy Kavkaz in Georgia.**

FROM MOUNTAIN PEAKS TO SWAMPY LOWLAND

Georgia can be roughly divided into three main geographical areas: the Great Caucasus range, the central lowlands, and the Lesser Caucasus.

THE GREAT CAUCASUS Higher than the Swiss Alps, the Great Caucasus range dominates the landscape of northern Georgia. The mountain belts rise from the east and are often separated by deep gorges.

The Bokovoy range is northernmost; farther south the most important spurs are those of the Lomisi and Kartli ranges. The cone of Mount Kazbek, an extinct volcano, dominates the Bokovoy range at a height of 16,558 feet (5,047 m). Georgia's spectacular crest-lined peaks also include Mount Shkhara (16,627 feet/5,066 m), Mount Tetnuldi (15,938 feet/4,858 m), and Mount Ushba (15,419 feet/4,700 m)—all in the region of

One of the numerous magnificent views offered by the Caucasus mountain range.

Upper Svaneti—and Mount Rustaveli (15,944 feet/4,860 m) to the southeast. The wooded gorges and valleys in bloom have been a great lure for writers and travelers throughout the ages, including Russian writers Alexander Pushkin, Mikhail Lermontov, Lev Nikolaevich Tolstoy, and Maxim Gorky, as well as French writer Alexandre Dumas.

Lermontov, for example, described the Krestovy Pass in his novel *A Hero of Our Time* (1840), writing, "What a delightful place, that valley! On all sides rise inaccessible mountains, reddish cliffs hung over with great ivy crowned with clumps of plane trees; tawny precipices streaked with washes, and far above the golden fringe of the snows. . . ."

Few roads traverse the Great Caucasus; the scenic Georgian Military Highway that links Georgia to Russia is the best known. Other routes over the mountain range include the Mamison Pass in Racha and the Klukhor Pass in Abkhazia.

THE GEORGIAN MILITARY HIGHWAY

The 128-mile (206-km) Georgian Military Highway cuts north through the Great Caucasus range to connect Georgia with Russia and beyond. Beginning in Tbilisi, this road crosses the precipitous mountains to reach Vladikavkaz in southern Russia. The route that began as a track used by invaders since the first century B.C. became part of the Silk Road. It provided an important trade link between Europe and Asia. For many centuries it was dangerous, and in winter it was often impassable. It rises to an impressive height of 7,983 feet (2,433 m) at the Krestovy Pass, which is actually the lowest and easiest route over the Caucasus. The route offers the traveler fantastic views of the surrounding mountains and river valleys.

Today's Georgian Military Highway was originally built by the Russians to improve communications with their new subject territory. It was completed in 1817 by the Russian regional commander General Alexie Yermelov (1772–1861), on the orders of Tsar Alexander I. The name of the route originates from this time, when the Russians used the road to move troops to aid their conquest of Transcaucasia.

The Georgian Military Highway is set on the mountain lowlands, connecting Tbilisi to the northern borders.

CENTRAL LOWLANDS The southern slopes of the Caucasus merge gradually into Georgia's central lowland areas. The Kolkhida lowlands are to the west, spreading from the shores of the Black Sea. Many of Georgia's major rivers rush down from the slopes of the Great Caucasus across the Kolkhida lowlands to the Black Sea. These include the Kodori, Enguri, and Rioni. The Rioni River is thought to be the Phasis of Greek legend, along which Jason and the Argonauts traveled to capture the Golden Fleece. At one time the lowlands were mostly swampland. A development program that constructed drainage canals and river embankments improved the region, so that it is now an important area for growing subtropical crops such as tea and citrus fruits. The climate in this region is hot and damp.

SVANETI

Upper and Lower Svaneti have the most inaccessible and difficult terrains in Georgia. Upper Svaneti (Zemo Svaneti) is wholly mountainous, with a small population of about 15,000. Lower Svaneti (Kvemo Svaneti) has a population of 12,000. Mestia, the chief town of Upper Svaneti, was not accessible by motor vehicles until 1935, when the road was widened with dynamite.

Situated 7,220 feet (2,200 m) above sea level in the region of Upper Svaneti, Ushguli is the highest continuously inhabited village in Europe. Like many other centers in Svaneti, the village is striking because of the more than 20 medieval watchtowers that dot its landscape. The surrounding mountain scenery is superb, with good views of the nearby peaks of Ushba and Shkhara.

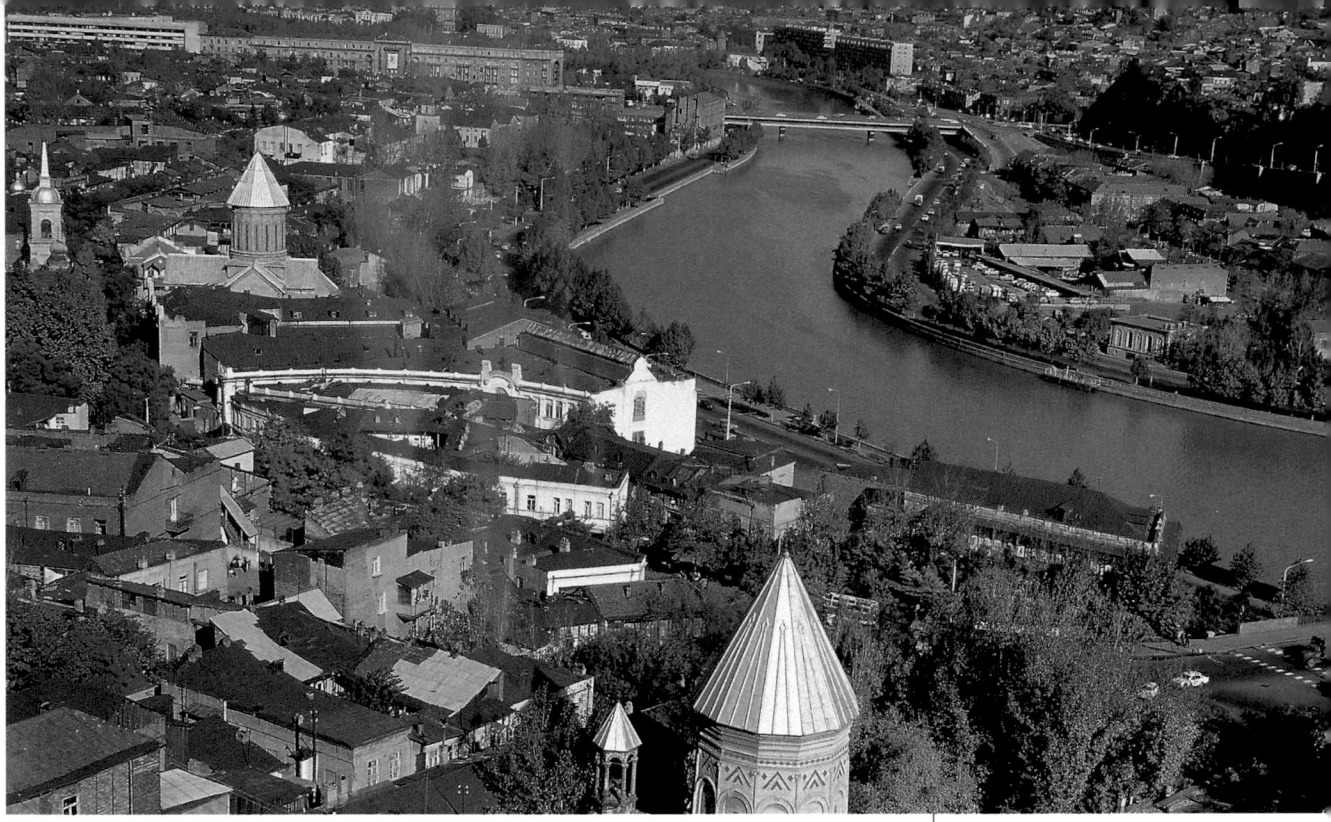

The densely populated urban areas of Tbilisi and Mtskheta are located in the Lesser Caucasus, close to neighboring Turkey, Armenia, and Azerbaijan.

The Likhi mountain range forms a bridge between the Great and Lesser Caucasus, and marks the division between the east and west of the country. To the west of the Likhi range, the Kartalinian Plain forms an arid plateau, situated between Khashuri and the ancient capital of Mtskheta. This central plateau extends along the Kura River and its tributaries. The Kura River is the longest one in Transcaucasia. It begins in northeast Turkey, passes through central Georgia, and runs the whole length of Azerbaijan before flowing into the Caspian Sea.

The easternmost part of Georgia is formed around the Alazani River Valley and the Iori Plateau, both of which are divided by the Gombori mountain range. The Alazani Valley is Georgia's chief grape-growing and winemaking region.

THE LESSER CAUCASUS Southern Georgia is marked by the ranges and plateaus of the Lesser Caucasus that divide Georgia from its southern neighbors, Turkey and Armenia. The highest peak of the Lesser Caucasus is Mount Didi-Abuli (10,830 feet/3,300 m). The mountains, almost completely covered with cedar and beech forests, resemble the temperate rain forests of British Columbia.

It is estimated that Tbilisi has been destroyed 29 times by different conquerors throughout the city's long and turbulent history.

Opposite: **The capital city of Tbilisi is an industrial area with an active private sector.**

REGIONS

Georgia is an ethnically diverse country, so regional identity is important to its various peoples. The country is divided into nine administrative regions; two autonomous republics, Abkhazia and Adjara; and one autonomous region, South Ossetia. The administrative regions are Guria, Imereti, Kakheti, Kvemo Kartli, Mtskheta-Mtianeti, Racha-Lechkhumi and Kvemo Svaneti, Samegrelo and Zemo Svaneti, Samtskhe-Javakheti, and Shida Kartli. These regions are subdivided into 65 districts.

Historically Imereti and Samegrelo formed the nucleus of western Georgia, while Kartli and Kakheti formed the rump of eastern Georgia. Regions such as Upper and Lower Svaneti, Khevi, and Khevsureti are mountainous and lightly populated.

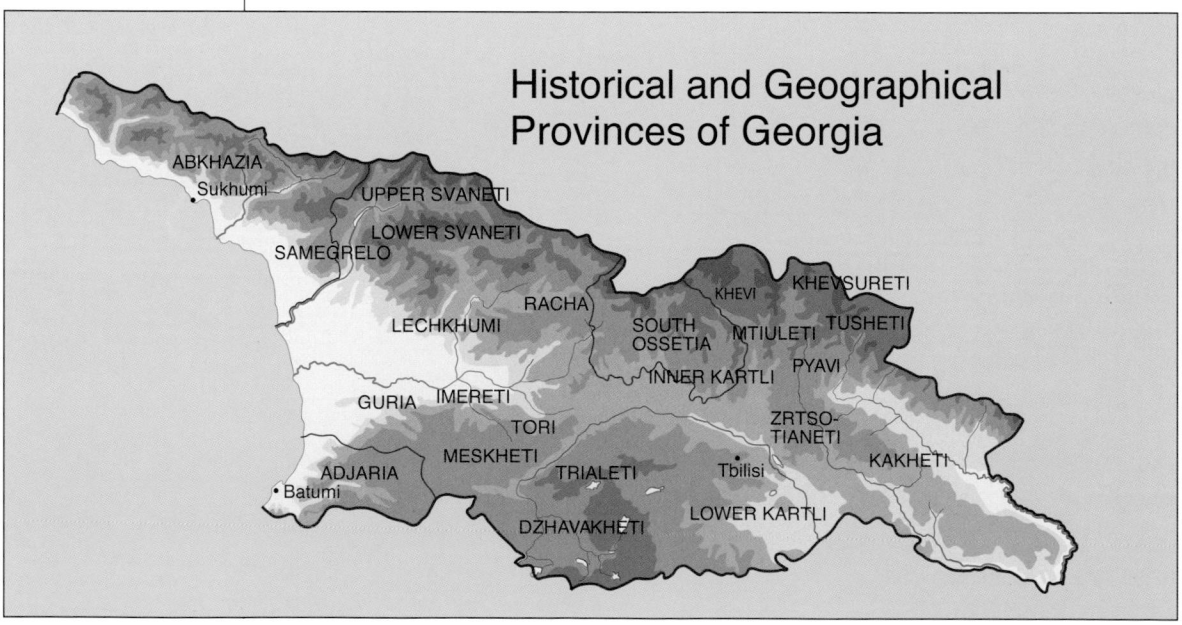

CITIES

TBILISI With a population of 1.3 million, Tbilisi (t-BLI-si), the capital of Georgia, is the country's most populous city. It is a long, narrow city that straddles both banks of the Kura River. The city is built on several hills and is protected on three sides by mountains.

Founded in A.D. 458 by King Vakhtang Gorgasali, Tbilisi was named after some nearby hot sulfur springs. The name *Tbilisi* means "warm." The city, situated at the crossroads between Asia and Europe, reflects the influences of both continents. Ruled by both Muslims and Christians at different times in its checkered history, Tbilisi has a cosmopolitan, multiethnic character that is reflected in its architecture, which ranges from the Moorish-style Opera House to medieval churches and Baroque Russian architecture.

The city's main, tree-lined thoroughfare, Rustaveli Avenue, is named after the 13th-century Georgian poet Shota Rustaveli. Georgians have always venerated their poets more than other artists.

Tbilisi is also an industrial city and accounts for more than 40 percent of the country's industrial output. It has had a subway system since 1966.

Gelati Monastery in Kutaisi was built in the 12th century by King David the Builder to celebrate his early victories against the Seljuk Turks.

KUTAISI Kutaisi is situated near the Rioni River in the central lowlands and is the capital of the Imereti region. It has a population of 250,000, making it the second largest city after Tbilisi. Legend has it that the capital city of King Aeëtes, custodian of the Golden Fleece, was situated here. The Rioni River—known in ancient times as the Phasis—is navigable all the way to the Black Sea, and would have allowed Jason and his Argonauts access to it. Kutaisi is known to have existed as a Greek colony in the seventh century B.C., and was the capital of Georgia from 978 to 1122. It contains impressive medieval structures such as the Cathedral of King Bagrat, Gelati Monastery, and the Monastery of Montsameta—all built during the "golden age" of King David the Builder and Queen Tamar.

OTHER CITIES Batumi (population 124,000), the capital of the autonomous region of Ajaria, is Georgia's most important port on the southern Black Sea coast. It began as a port under the Romans and reached its height of prominence in the Middle Ages, but was devastated by the Turks in the 16th century. Modern Batumi is a city of parks with subtropical vegetation, a broad stony beach, and high-rise tourist hotels. Despite the town's wet climate, it is a popular holiday resort, especially with Russian tourists.

Sukhumi (population 112,000), the capital of the autonomous region of Abkhazia, is situated on the Bay of Sukhumi. Like Batumi it is a popular resort town; unlike its southern counterpart, however, it has a sunny climate.

Other major towns include Rustavi (Georgia's main industrial center), Poti, Khashuri, Tskhinvali (the chief town of South Ossetia), and Gori.

A typical Georgian winter, with the roads covered by thick snow.

CLIMATE

Georgia has a varied climate, ranging from subtropical humidity to snow and ice. The Great Caucasus forms a barrier that protects Georgia from cold air from the north, while the west of the country is open to warm, moist air from the Black Sea.

Western Georgia has a damp subtropical climate with heavy rainfall all year. The rain is heaviest around Batumi in the south. Winters in the west are mild and warm, and the temperature never falls below 32°F (0°C). Along the Black Sea coast, the temperature rarely falls below 40°F (4°C).

Eastern Georgia is cut off from the warm air of the Black Sea by the Likhi mountain range and consequently has a drier, more continental climate. Altitude also exerts an important climatic influence. Most of the Caucasus is above 6,000 feet (1,800 m) and has an Alpine climate, lacking a true summer. Many of eastern Georgia's mountains are over 11,000 feet (3,300 m) above sea level and are covered with snow most of the year.

FLORA AND FAUNA

"Nature here is astounding to the point of despair. If I lived in Abkhazia for as much as a month, I think I'd write half a hundred exquisite tales."

—*From a letter by the Russian playwright Anton Chekhov*

Georgia's varied landscape has created an unusual diversity of flora. There are 5,000 types of mushroom, 2,000 types of seaweed, nearly 600 types of moss, and 73 varieties of fern. Forests and brush cover more than one-third of Georgia, and the vegetation varies from east to west. Georgia has between 4,000 and 4,500 species of vascular plants.

Some flora in western Georgia is subtropical. Alder trees predominate in the swampy coastal areas of the Kolkhida lowlands. Farther inland, where the climate is drier, the forests include oak, chestnut, beech, and liana. The Pitsunda pine can be found in Abkhazia. A grove of these unique trees is protected in a national park on the Pitsunda Cape.

Forests and lush greenery dot Georgia's mountains and grasslands.

PHEASANTS (PHASIANUS COLCHICUS)

Pheasants are indigenous throughout the Caucasus and southeastern Europe. They are larger than quail or partridge, and most are long-tailed birds of the open woodlands and fields, although some prefer grain fields near brushy cover. All pheasants have hoarse calls and a variety of other call-notes. The males of most pheasant species are strikingly colored, while the females are more inconspicuous. Courting males sometimes fight to the death in the presence of hens.

Many pheasants are kept in private collections and are also raised for sport in some game reserves. Some species have been brought to the verge of extinction by hunting. Legend has it that Jason and the Argonauts first introduced pheasants to Greece (and from there to the rest of Europe) when they returned home from their arduous adventures. It is thought that the name *pheasant* derives from the River Phasis, now called the Rioni River, down which the Argonauts traveled when they escaped from Colchis with the Golden Fleece.

Eastern Georgia has fewer forests and is dominated by grasslands dotted with prickly undergrowth. The lowlands and foothills are forested only along the rivers, especially the Kura, Iori, and Alazani, where oak, poplar, and willow trees can be found. In the higher, wetter regions, juniper, pomegranate, Georgian maple, and pistachio trees grow well.

Georgia's unique geographical location has resulted in a mixture of European and Asian fauna, with 100 mammal, 330 bird, 48 reptile, 11 amphibian, and 160 fish species. There are gazelles, deer, and wild boars in eastern Georgia's lowlands. The goitered gazelle and dwarf shrew, both endangered species, can be found only around Tbilisi.

The western lowlands of the country have a greater diversity of fauna. A variety of mammals such as moles, squirrels, brown bears, badgers, weasels, deer, wolves, foxes, lynx, mink, and wildcats can be found here. Birds of this region include pheasants, geese, curlews, ducks, cormorants, and woodpeckers, and, during times of migration, pelicans, storks, herons, hawks, and eagle owls.

The Alpine areas of Georgia are inhabited by many species of birds, including the Caucasian jackdaw, black grouse, pheasant, cuckoo, woodpecker, and magpie. Goats and Caucasian antelope can also be found in the mountains, and the rivers are full of trout. The Black Sea has a rich diversity of sea life, including dolphins, sharks, salmon, herring, dogfish, and swordfish.

Georgia has one of the largest proportions of land dedicated to national parks (25 percent) in the world (by contrast, the United States has only 4 percent of its land protected). Georgia has 31 national parks and protected areas identified for conservation.

HISTORY

MANY PEOPLE THINK of Georgia as a small part of the former Soviet Empire, not realizing that it has a rich and ancient history of its own. Georgia is situated at a geographical crossroads between Europe and Asia. As a result it shares the complicated and turbulent history of the Middle East.

This fiercely independent Caucasian republic has often been dominated by greater neighboring powers—Byzantium, Persia, Turkey, and most recently Russia—all of which have left their marks. Despite these influences, however, Georgia has retained an uninterrupted and powerful national identity, culture, and language.

EARLY HISTORY

Remains of an anthropoid ape discovered in Georgia suggest that the Caucasus was one of the birthplaces of human life. Archaeological excavations and the discovery of cave drawings along the Black Sea coast suggest human existence around the Middle Paleolithic period (150,000–40,000 B.C.). Paleolithic man lived in caves or earth dugouts and survived mainly by hunting animals and gathering fruits and berries. A Neolithic culture existed in Georgia from 5000 to 4000 B.C. The Neolithic inhabitants were hunters, fishers, and food gatherers.

Bronze Age man thrived in Georgia between the third and second millennia B.C. It was at about this time that Georgian metallurgy developed and Georgian metalworkers became the most renowned in the ancient world.

Above: **An illustration of a Turkish storyteller in the days when the Turks ruled vast areas of Transcaucasia.**

Opposite: **Statues of Georgia's founding pioneers stand before the parliament building.**

An ancient carving (c. fifth to eighth centuries B.C.) on stone from the Iberian period in Georgia.

At the end of the third millennium B.C., the Kurgan people invaded the Caucasus from the Eurasian grasslands. Elements of this Kurgan culture fused with the cultures of the local people to form the famous Trialeti culture in the region southwest of Tbilisi. Remarkable finds in Trialeti show that it was inhabited by cattle-raising tribes whose chieftains were men of power and wealth. Burial mounds have been discovered that date from 2100 to 1500 B.C. Many of them contain vessels of gold and silver.

COLCHIS AND GREECE

The historical records of the Assyrians provide the first concrete evidence of the rulers and tribes of Georgia. The western part of Georgia, then known as Colchis, is famous in ancient history and mythology. It was first mentioned in Assyrian records in the 12th century B.C. From the eighth century B.C. on, the place had been visited by the ancient Greeks, who set up colonies and trading stations all around the Black Sea.

THE IBERIANS

Around 730 B.C. the Cimmerians and Scythians from the north attacked Georgia and occupied Colchis and much of the Caucasus. Their invasions scattered many of the ancestral tribes of Georgia into the more remote mountain regions, and pushed some of them into the Persian sphere of influence. However, the Tibareni and Mushki tribes managed to reestablish themselves in eastern Georgia by the time Alexander the Great of Macedonia crushed the Persians at the Battle of Arbela in 331 B.C.

The two tribes then merged with local tribes to form the kingdom of Iberia, with its capital at Mtskheta. Here, for the first time, a common Georgian language was developed, and Mtskheta, situated 20 miles (32 km) north of modern-day Tbilisi, thrived at the crossroads of a busy trade route that linked Greece to the west with India and China to the east.

In 66 B.C. the Romans, under the command of Pompey, conquered Iberia. The resulting Roman influence brought many advantages to the Iberians, including new roads and increased trade with the rest of the Roman Empire. Soon Iberia established such good relations with the Romans that Iberia was considered an ally rather than a subject state.

CONVERSION TO CHRISTIANITY

The Iberians embraced Christianity in A.D. 330 during the reign of the Roman Emperor Constantine the Great. The conversion is attributed to Saint Nino, a woman who was said to possess healing powers. Political conditions favored the adoption of the new religion—it was the official creed of the still-powerful Romans, and neighboring Armenia had converted 30 years earlier. In the fifth century A.D. King Vakhtang Gorgasali (reigned 446–510) strengthened the Iberian Church by establishing an independent bishop at Mtskheta, which remains the center of the Georgian Orthodox Church today. The king also moved his capital to Tbilisi in 458, thus founding the capital city.

To the west of Iberia, Lazica—a kingdom that had sprung up from the ruins of Colchis—adopted Christianity in the sixth century. For much of the sixth and seventh centuries, Lazica and Iberia found themselves at the center of a power struggle between Byzantium to the west and Persia to the east. The struggle ended when the Arabs, inspired by the new Islamic faith, swept through Persia and the entire region, capturing Tbilisi in 645.

The Byzantine and Persian empires fought over Georgia between the sixth and seventh centuries. Genghis Khan invaded in 1220, and Turkey and Persia sparred over Georgia in the 16th century. Four centuries later, in 1921, Soviet armies invaded the country, and Georgia remained a part of the Soviet Union until it declared its independence on April 9, 1991.

THE ARGONAUTS' QUEST FOR THE GOLDEN FLEECE

The earliest version of this legend was told by Apollonius Rhodius in his epic poem *Argonautica*, composed in the third century B.C. Greek geographer Strabo (63 B.C.–A.D. 23) also tells of the Golden Fleece in his literary work *Geography*. Many details in the *Argonautica* have since been supported by archaeological evidence, suggesting that the Argonauts' journey may be more than just a legend.

According to the story, a Greek prince named Jason set out with a band of 50 men in a ship called the *Argo* to find the fabled Golden Fleece. His uncle, Pelias, had usurped the throne belonging to his father, and Jason could only regain his rightful crown by proving his bravery. In the search for the Golden Fleece, the Argonauts encountered many dangers during a long and eventful journey that finally took them to Colchis.

There Aeëtes, the Colchian king, refused to give up the Golden Fleece unless Jason went through several trials. First he had to tame the king's fire-snorting bulls and yoke them to a plow, which Jason achieved through strength and cunning. Next he had to plow a field and plant a helmet full of dragon's teeth, each of which sprang up into armed warriors, whom he then had to defeat. Aeëtes's daughter Medea, a sorceress who had fallen in love with Jason, stepped in to help. She advised him to throw a stone among the warriors, causing confusion so that they turned in anger upon one another and fought to the death, leaving Jason victorious.

Aeëtes, however, still refused to part with the Golden Fleece, which was being guarded by an ever-watchful dragon. Once again Medea went to Jason's aid. She guided him to the Fleece and cast a spell on the dragon, causing it to fall asleep. This allowed Jason to escape in the *Argo* with both the Golden Fleece and Medea.

Constantinople was the capital of the powerful Byzantine Empire, which fought against the Arabs for control of the Georgian region, previously known as Iberia.

ARAB DOMINATION

The Arabs were not interested in colonizing Georgia, and Georgian culture and Christian religion were allowed to flourish. Georgian princes were allowed to rule, but under Arab supervision. Tbilisi soon became the center of several important international trade routes that dealt with goods from Russia, Daghestan, and the Middle East.

In the ninth century the Bagratid clan came into prominence. The Bagratids would unite Georgia under a single crown and hold power for the next 1,000 years. Their rule ended only with Russian annexation in 1801. The first Bagratid ruler, King Ashot I (reigned 813–30), was appointed ruler of much of southern Georgia. Under King Bagrat III (reigned 975–1014), the eastern and western parts of Georgia became unified for the first time. It is only from this time that Georgia can be referred to as the single entity we know of today. Under King Bagrat IV (reigned 1027–72), Georgia became one of the most powerful states in the Caucasus.

King Giorgi II could not cope with Turkish threats and handed over the running of the kingdom to his son.

DAVID THE BUILDER

In the 11th century the Seljuk Turks pushed westward, capturing Persia and Armenia and invading Byzantium. The Byzantine Army was crushed at Manzikert in 1071. Later the son of King Bagrat IV, King Giorgi II, reigned from 1072 until 1089, when, unable to deal with the onslaught of the Turks, he abdicated the throne. His 16-year-old son, David (1073–1125), took over.

Under King David, who was known as The Builder, national unity was restored, and trade, culture, and religion flourished. King David resisted the Turks, winning many brilliant victories between 1110 and 1122, and defeating the Turks decisively at the Battle of Didgori in 1121. Tbilisi was recaptured from the Turks in 1122. The king's humane treatment of the Turkish Muslim population set a standard of tolerance in his multiethnic kingdom.

King David also managed to extend Georgia's territory as far as the Caspian Sea, and he captured parts of Armenia as well. His campaigns were indirectly aided by the timely arrival of the European Crusaders in Palestine. The Crusaders captured the Holy Land in 1099 and were a constant threat to the Islamic world over the next few centuries, allowing Georgia to develop its own culture and reinforce and extend its borders without Arab interference. (The term *Holy Land* generally refers to Israel and the historic geographical region of Palestine. It concerns the areas that hold significant religious importance to the three monotheistic Abrahamic religions: Judaism, Christianity, and Islam.)

QUEEN TAMAR

The great works of King David were continued by his great-granddaughter, Queen Tamar (reigned 1184–1212). Christian culture flourished, and many religious buildings were constructed, among them the Vardzia Caves. With the fall of the Byzantine Empire to the Muslims in 1204, Queen Tamar was able to extend the boundaries of Georgia westward along the Black Sea coast and create the independent empire of Trebizond. Under Queen Tamar the Georgian feudal system reached its zenith and the virtues of chivalry and honor were celebrated in Shota Rustaveli's (1172–1216) epic romance, *The Knight in the Panther's Skin.*

Portrait of Queen Tamar found in the Vardzia Caves in the Lesser Caucasus.

THE MONGOL YOKE

The Mongol invasion of Transcaucasia in 1220 brought Georgia's "golden age" to an end. Led by Genghis Khan, the Mongols swept across much of Asia and eventually threatened the borders of Europe. The Mongols were an aggressive, well-armed, and well-trained army of horsemen who were notorious for their cruelty and bravery. Queen Tamar's heir, King Giorgi IV Lasha (reigned 1213–22), was killed in a battle against the Mongols. The Mongols dominated Georgia for the next century, taxing the Georgians heavily.

King Giorgi V (reigned 1314–46), who was called "The Brilliant," took advantage of weakening Mongol power to regain Georgian independence. Unfortunately the Central Asian conqueror, Tamerlane (1336–1405), in the course of his campaigns against the Turks and Persians, caused much havoc and destruction from which the kingdom never fully recovered. Georgia was overrun on eight consecutive occasions; towns and churches were ruined, and the people fled to the hills.

A 19th-century engraving of Abbas I, shah of the Persian Empire.

OTTOMAN TURKEY AND SAFAVID PERSIA

In 1453 the Ottoman Turks captured Constantinople, isolating Georgia from European Christendom. At the end of the 15th century the rise of the Safavid Persians posed a further threat to Georgia, which found itself caught once more between two expanding empires to the east and west. Both the Turks and Persians encroached upon Georgian territory until, in the Peace of Amasia in 1555, Georgia was divided into spheres of influence—the Turks controlled western Georgia while the Persians controlled the eastern part. The Georgians were powerless to resist.

In 1578 the Turks overran the whole of Transcaucasia, but were subsequently driven out by the Persian Shah Abbas I (reigned 1557–1628). The Georgian people were heavily persecuted for their Christian beliefs, and many were deported to distant regions of Persia (present-day Iran), where their descendants can still be found today. Queen Ketevan of Kakheti was given the choice of abandoning the Christian faith and entering the shah's harem, or suffering a cruel martyrdom. She chose to die for her faith, and is numbered among the saints of the Georgian Church. For the next 200 years the kings of Kartli, as eastern Georgia was then known, ruled only through the will of the Persian shahs.

RUSSIAN ANNEXATION

In the early 18th century the Bagratid kings Taimuraz II (reigned 1744–62) and Herekle II (reigned 1762–98) were able to rebuild Georgia in its own image, not Persia's. Persian power was waning, and the Russians were expanding into Transcaucasia. Nevertheless Persian-backed Muslim raiders from north of the Caucasus and Daghestan had a crippling effect on Georgian trade and industry. It is estimated that the population of Georgia might have been reduced by as much as half by the end of the 18th century because of these attacks. King Herekle II, convinced that his isolated Christian kingdom could not hold out against an assortment of Muslim enemies, sought the aid of Christian Russia.

In 1783 Russia and Georgia signed the Treaty of Georgievsk. Under the agreement Georgia became a Russian protectorate, renouncing all dependence on Persia. Despite Russian promises of protection, Tbilisi was sacked again in 1795 by the Persians, and 50,000 of its inhabitants were killed. Herekle II, the 75-year-old king, fought in the battle and narrowly escaped capture. He died in 1798.

In 1800 Herekle II's son, the invalid King Giorgi XII, decided to hand over the kingdom to the care of the Russians unconditionally in exchange for their full protection. The king died that same year. He was the last ruler of the 1,000-year-old Bagratid Dynasty. In 1801 the Russian Tsar Alexander I confirmed that Kartli and Kakheti were a part of the Russian Empire and abolished the Bagratid monarchy. The western realm (Imereti) ruled by Solomon II continued until 1810, only to meet the same fate.

Tsar Alexander I's expansionist program brought numerous regions of western Georgia under Russian rule.

GEORGIA UNDER THE TSARS

Under Tsar Alexander I, the Russians continued their expansion into the Caucasus, waging war against the Turks, Persians, and the Lezgian tribesmen of Daghestan. Russian power brought stability to Georgia, and under the guidance of the gifted and enlightened Russian viceroy Michael Vorontsov (1782–1856), industry and trade prospered, and communications improved. In 1872 a railway was built to link Tbilisi with Poti, and Russian and Western entrepreneurs developed plantations.

With increased communication, however, came change. The Russian social administration replaced the old Georgian feudal system, and Russian education and culture became widespread. Many Georgian intellectuals reacted against Russian influence. The "Men of the 1860s" were a group of radicals and social activists, full of the new social democratic ideals that were then current in Europe. Although tsarist Russia did not permit any organized political activity, social issues were debated in journals and local assemblies, and through works of fiction.

The 1890s saw the appearance of a new group of radicals who had absorbed the political ideals of Karl Marx, a revolutionary Communist from Germany, while studying abroad. They were called the *tergdaleulni* (terg-dal-e-UL-ni), meaning "those who had drunk from the river Terek," an act that symbolized their going out into the world, beyond the boundaries of Georgia. The leader of this group was Noe Zhordania (1868–1953). Another prominent member was Joseph Dzhugashvili, better known as Joseph Stalin.

Soldiers of the 1917 revolution, when the Bolsheviks seized power from the tsarist authorities in Russia.

WAR AND REVOLUTION A failed 1905 revolution in Russia led to social unrest and industrial strikes in Georgia. These were brutally suppressed by Cossacks, a group in southern Russia that fought for the tsarist army. In 1914 Russia entered World War I, fighting against the Germans and Austrians. The Russian Army collapsed in 1917, amid economic disintegration, severe food shortages, and social upheaval at home. This was followed by one of the 20th century's most momentous events: the Russian Revolution, which began in November 1917. Under the leadership of Vladimir Lenin (1870–1924), the Bolsheviks, a faction of the Marxist Russian Social Democratic Labour Party (RSDLP) that split apart from the Menshevik faction at the Second Party Congress in 1903 and ultimately became the Communist Party of the Soviet Union, seized power.

In Georgia the power vacuum was filled by the Social Democratic Party, led by Noe Zhordania. The country regained its autonomy for the first time in 117 years and maintained a neutral stance throughout the Russian civil war, from 1917 to 1920, but its independence was short-lived. In February 1921, following victories throughout Russia, the Bolshevik 11th Red Army marched into Georgia, driving Zhordania and his government into exile. Georgia was once more in the grip of its more powerful neighbor.

JOSEPH STALIN (1879–1953)

Perhaps the most famous and notorious Georgian of modern times, Stalin was born in Gori, Inner Kartli. Originally christened Joseph Vissarionovich Dzhugashvili, he adopted the name *Stalin*, meaning "man of steel" (in Russian), when he entered revolutionary politics. Stalin's family was poor and his father was a drunkard. Despite great hardship, his mother succeeded in sending Stalin to an Orthodox seminary in Tbilisi, where he trained for the priesthood. He was expelled in 1899; it is suspected that this was because he was propagating Marxism.

Although he was anti-tsarist, Stalin was never a nationalist. He did not believe that Georgia's salvation lay in independence, but rather in becoming part of a larger political structure. He became active in Georgia's revolutionary underground. He was arrested and imprisoned many times and exiled to Siberia twice by the tsarist authorities. He became friends with Lenin and was at the forefront of the 1917 Bolshevik Revolution. When Lenin died in 1924, Stalin had so much power that he was able to isolate and disgrace his political rivals. In 1928 he exiled his main political rival, Leon Trotsky (1879–1940), and gained absolute control of the Communist Party.

Stalin was a cruel, ruthless, and dictatorial ruler who was responsible for the imprisonment or death of many millions of people in the Soviet Union through forced collectivization and political purges in the 1930s. It is estimated that as many as 20 million Soviet citizens died as a result of his policies. Nevertheless he gained a reputation as a great war leader, leading the Soviet Union to victory over the Germans in World War II. He died on March 5, 1953, under mysterious circumstances, probably from a brain hemorrhage.

SOVIET GEORGIA

Georgia was initially incorporated into the Transcaucasian Soviet Federated Republic in 1922, along with Armenia and Azerbaijan. The Georgian Social Democrats, still popular despite their earlier defeat, organized a rebellion in 1924 that was put down by the Red Army. Seven thousand people were executed, and Soviet rule was finally established in Georgia.

In 1936 Georgia became one of the 15 republics of the Soviet Union. Joseph Stalin, a native Georgian, ruled the Soviet Union from 1928 to 1953. Despite the fact that he and his chief of police, Lavrenti Beria (1899–1953), were Georgians, Stalin treated his homeland harshly.

During World War II (1939–45) the Georgians helped defend the Soviet Union against the German invasion of the northern Caucasus. German paratroopers were dropped into Georgia to aid the German advance, but

In 1945, after the defeat of Nazi Germany, it was a Georgian soldier, with a Russian comrade, who hoisted the Soviet red flag over the seat of German power, the Reichstag.

they were promptly caught by the local militia. The German advance was thus stemmed.

Soviet economic policy forced the collectivization—a policy adopted by the Soviet government and pursued most intensively between 1929 and 1933 to transform traditional agriculture in the Soviet Union and to reduce the economic power of the prosperous peasants—of all agricultural workers, as had happened throughout the Soviet Union. Georgia was converted from a largely agricultural economy into an industrial and urban society.

Following Stalin's death in 1953, a freewheeling "second economy" developed, providing goods and services that were not available in the planned state economy. Far from the center of power in Moscow, most Georgians were able to grow their own crops privately and run their own cottage industries. Older Georgians still look back to the 1960s and 1970s with great nostalgia. It was a time of public order, peace, and high standards of living.

Despite current economic difficulties, these small cottage industries started during the Soviet era remain fundamental to the Georgian economy and lifestyle even today.

A child places his grandmother's vote into a sealed box at a polling station.

RECENT HISTORY

In the late 1980s the Soviet Union underwent fundamental political and social changes under the leadership of Mikhail Gorbachev (b. 1931). In the new atmosphere of glasnost (openness), political and social freedoms were reinstated.

In April 1989 demonstrations held in Tbilisi to demand independence were brutally suppressed by Soviet special troops, and 20 civilians were killed. After the tragic event, however, the massacre was reported by the Soviet authorities to have been a mistake. Soviet President Gorbachev had not ordered the suppression; the decision had been made by the local government and army commanders. It was partly due to this event that the Soviets began to lose control over Georgia: Anti-Soviet sentiment was fueled by the suppression, and this speeded up the move toward independence. There was little that the Soviet authorities could do other than launch a full military invasion, which would have been highly impractical and unpopular in the unstable social and political climate of the time.

Soon new political parties appeared. Free elections held in 1990 were won by a coalition called the Round Table, led by a former dissident named Zviad Gamsakhurdia (1939–94). Georgia was declared independent on April 9, 1991, and Gamsakhurdia was elected president of the new republic. His authoritarian rule made him unpopular, however. Civil war broke out in late 1991, and a military council deposed him in 1992. The military council soon handed power to a state council made up of various political parties that were headed by Eduard Shevardnadze (b. 1928). Shevardnadze had served as Soviet foreign minister under Gorbachev. Despite terrorist attempts to kill him in August

1995, elections held in November of that same year confirmed him as president for five years. In 2000 he emerged victorious yet again in the presidential elections.

The Soviet Union disintegrated in 1991, and the Commonwealth of Independent States (CIS) was formed, consisting of 15 newly independent countries of the former Soviet Union. Georgia joined the CIS in 1993.

Life for independent Georgia has not been peaceful or trouble-free, and the nation still has much to do in order to establish stability in one of the most volatile regions in the world. In South Ossetia rebels have been fighting a war for independence against Georgian forces; they seek unification with North Ossetia in Russia. In Abkhazia sporadic fighting has continued since 1992. Near Georgia's borders, conflicts continue in Nagorno-Karabakh between Georgia's neighbors Azerbaijan and Armenia, and an uneasy peace has held since the end of 1996 in neighboring Chechnya. The Rose Revolution of 2003 brought down the government led by Eduard Shevardnadze, who was accused of corruption, and swept Mikhail Saakashvili, a United States–educated lawyer and former justice minister into power. At the age of 35 Saakashvili became Europe's youngest president in early 2004. The new president spared no time in reforming Georgia's military, bringing it closer to the standards required to become a member of the North Atlantic Treaty Organization (NATO), an organization whose members give one another military aid when necessary.

Fighting in Chechnya has contributed to the climate of instability in the Caucasus.

GOVERNMENT

GEORGIA HAS HAD LITTLE political stability since it gained its independence in April 1991. For the first time in 70 years, it was free and self-governing, and many Georgians wanted a strong, centralized state to reinforce this newfound independence. Unfortunately ethnic unrest and separatist revolts have resulted in a turbulent political situation. The Georgian republic includes two autonomous republics and one autonomous region: the Abkhazian Autonomous Republic, the Adjarian Autonomous Republic, and the South Ossetian Autonomous Region. These regions were originally formed by the Soviet administration as semi-independent homelands for ethnic minorities. They have limited self-government, but have proved to be hotbeds of ethnic tension and conflict for the fledgling Georgian republic. It is estimated that more than 20,000 people have died in regional and ethnic conflicts in Georgia since 1991.

Above: **Abkhazian refugees awaiting evacuation by the United Nations.**

Opposite: **The entrance to the parliament house in Thilisi**

RECENT EVENTS

For 70 years Georgia was a part of the Soviet Union and had no independent government of its own. A Georgian parliament did exist—the Georgian Supreme Soviet—but as the national branch of the Communist Party, it could only implement decisions that were made centrally by the Communist Party leaders in Moscow.

Amid the disintegration of the Soviet Union, free elections were held in 1990 and Zviad Gamsakhurdia emerged victorious. However, his dictatorial methods led to his swift exit from power in early 1992.

Eduard Shevardnadze, the chairperson of the state council, was temporarily elected and an emergency constitution passed. Gamsakhurdia continued his opposition to the new government before dying under mysterious circumstances in early 1994. Shevardnadze was democratically elected as Georgia's leader in presidential elections held on November 5, 1995, and was reelected in 2000. A shrewd politician with vast international experience, he sought to modernize Georgia and forge closer economic ties with the West and the other newly independent republics in the Caucasus and Central Asia. Having served as foreign minister in Mikhail Gorbachev's Soviet administration during the 1980s, his international stature has ensured that Georgia's problems are gaining attention from other world leaders. Between 1992 and 1993 Abkhzia and South Ossetia achieved de facto independence from Georgia amid widespread interethnic violence and wars. Abkhaz separatists forced more than 250,000 Georgians, including Chechens, to leave Abkhazia.

Shevardnadze resigned following widespread allegations of ballot fraud in the parliamentary election of November 2003. Thousands of peaceful protesters carried roses through the streets of Tbilisi. This became known as the Rose Revolution. Mikhail Saakashvili of the National Movement came to power in January 2004. A United States–educated lawyer and former justice minister, President Saakashvili had campaigned on a platform of restoring integrity and improving relations with Russia. A series of reforms was launched to strengthen Georgia's military and economic capabilities.

Corruption was significantly reduced during the Saakashvili administration. The Corruption Perception Index rated Georgia joint 99th in the world in 2006, a great improvement from being joint 130th the year before. Georgia was also ranked Partly Free in the 2007 edition of *Freedom in the World*, Freedom House's annual survey of political rights and civil liberties worldwide. However, on November 7, a state of emergency was declared following clashes between the police and 50,000 to 100,000 protesters calling for the ousting of President Saakashvili. The protesters initially called for changes in the dates of planned elections and in the electoral system.Saakashvili rejected their demands and accused their leaders of serving the Kremlin. The opposition-led protesters then made his resignation their central aim.

THE 1995 CONSTITUTION

Prior to the elections in 1995, a new constitution was drawn up, based on many of the main principles of the country's 1921 constitution. The new constitution confirmed Georgia as a democratic state in which all citizens are equal. The constitution protects basic human rights such as freedom of speech and thought, freedom of religious practice, and the freedom to own property.

THE GEORGIAN FLAG

The medieval flag of Georgia was adopted by the new government on January 14, 2004, when Mikhail Saakashvili won the presidential election. It has a single red cross on a white background in the center and four smaller crosses in the white quarters. The flag symbolizes Jesus Christ and the four evangelists Matthew, Mark, Luke, and John. The white background is a sign of innocence, chastity, purity, and wisdom. The red color of the cross represents courage, bravery, justice, and love.

The parliament house in Tbilisi.

PARLIAMENT

The Georgian parliament is a unicameral body consisting of 235 members elected by proportional representation—85 are elected to single-member seats and 150 are elected by proportional representation from party lists. Each member is elected for a four-year period. Parliament and other main government ministries are situated in the Government House of the Republic of Georgia, in the center of Tbilisi. Citizens must be at least 18 years old to vote in national elections, and 25 years old to run as deputies.

The president, as head of state, is elected for a term of five years and cannot serve more than two terms. He chooses his Council of Ministers (also known as a cabinet) and, along with the ministers, holds supreme executive power.

POLITICAL PARTIES

The Communist Party of Georgia was disbanded in 1991 following the collapse of the Soviet Union. Dozens of political parties were then formed, based mainly on regional or nationalist loyalties, or kinship ties. Often they had military backing from paramilitary or neogovernment groups.

President Mikhail Saakashvili's party, the National Movement, has enjoyed widespread popularity since 2004. Still, opposition parties are free to organize and campaign for office.

Georgians celebrating their state independence on May 26.

Refugees from the armed conflict in South Ossetia.

CONFLICTS IN ABKHAZIA AND SOUTH OSSETIA

The Abkhazians have been actively campaigning for independence for their region, the Abkhazian Autonomous Republic, since 1989. The Abkhazians have been in the region for 2,000 years and are ethnically different from Georgians. They are predominantly Orthodox Christians (75 percent), with Sunni Muslims making up approximately 10 percent. The Abkhazians have their own language. Through successive waves of migration during the 19th and 20th centuries, they have become a minority in their own homeland and now make up only 18 percent of the population.

In August 1990 Abkhazia's parliament, without its Georgian members, voted to separate from Georgia. However, the Georgian government ignored the declaration. In 1992 Abkhazian troops seized much of northern Abkhazia. A ceasefire was eventually established with the help of the United Nations (UN) and Russian mediation. In September 1993 Abkhazian separatist troops violated the ceasefire by sweeping southward capturing Sukhumi. Georgian government forces were driven out of the region, and the separatists declared Abkhazia liberated from Georgia. As a result 270,000 ethnic Georgians fled Abkhazia to western Georgia.

A number of United Nations–led negotiations have since been held, but to date there has been no settlement. The conflict has so far been contained within the borders of Georgia, but it has the potential to spill over and destabilize the entire region. Abkhazia is deemed an autonomous area, but this is to some extent merely a title, since no other state recognizes its sovereignty. In July 2006 Georgia disarmed the militia at Kodori Gorge and placed it under Georgian control. About 2,000 Russian peacekeeping troops are stationed in Abkhazia, but Tbilisi has called for a neutral international force to replace them.

An American charity supplies food and household goods to an Abkhazian refugee.

In the South Ossetian Autonomous Region, Ossetians have also been campaigning for separation. In 1989 the people demonstrated in support of Abkhazian separatist demands. The Ossetians speak their own language and most of them are Christians, though there is a sizable Muslim minority. They want greater control over their own affairs and, eventually, they

UNDER ARMS

Before 1991 Georgia's security was provided by the Soviet Army, in which many Georgians served as conscripts. Following independence two distinct military groups emerged in Georgia. The National Guard was formed to support the government, while a group called the Mkhedrioni (m-ked-RIO-ni), led by Dzahba Iosseliani, was formed to fight against the secessionist Abkhazians. However, the Mkhedrioni, numbering 7,000 men, soon developed into an independent force that was answerable only to their leader.

As a newcomer to the political scene, Shevardnadze was unable to control these groups when he first came to power in 1992. In 1995 the Mkhedrioni was implicated in an attempt to assassinate Shevardnadze. Since then it has lost much of its power and has, to some extent, been kept in check by the increasing stability of Shevardnadze's government. Today it still carries out illegal activities, but no longer operates as a government-sanctioned military force.

A regular Georgian Army has developed only gradually and faces many difficulties. Georgia had a total of 38,857 people in its armed forces in 2005, which were made up of the National Guard, the Navy, and Air Force. Military service is compulsory for two years for males above 18 years of age. There are up to 250,000 reservists, all of whom have completed national conscription. Defense spending was 0.59 percent of the nation's gross domestic product (GDP).

would like to unite with North Ossetia, which is part of the Russian Federation. The South Ossetian legislature declared itself an independent republic in 1990, in an attempt to have equal status with Georgia within the former Soviet Union. However, the Georgian parliament refused to recognize the Ossetian declaration of independence.

In 1991 the Ossetian parliament passed a resolution in favor of integration into the Russian Federation. Tensions led to violent clashes between Ossetians and ethnic Georgians in the region, and Georgian government troops were involved. Several thousand people were killed, and many South Ossetians fled across the border to North Ossetia to escape the violence. In 1992 a ceasefire was declared. This ceasefire, which was established with Russian participation, has been observed up to the present day. The Ossetian conflict is difficult to resolve. The Ossetians want unification with North Ossetia, while Georgians refuse to accept the loss of what they consider to be a part of their traditional homeland. In 1993 South Ossetia approved a constitution that established the region as a republic. Although it is not internationally recognized, it elected its own president in 1996. In January 2005 President Saakashvili proposed autonomous status for South Ossetia within Georgia in a bid to resolve the conflict.

ADJARIA—HAVEN OF STABILITY

Adjaria (also spelled Ajaria) has been Georgia's least troubled self-governing region since independence, and has not seen the extensive and bloody conflicts experienced in Abkhazia and South Ossetia. Despite their ethnic Georgian origin, the Adjarians retain a strong sense of separate identity, mainly because of their adherence to Islam. Most Georgians in the region converted to Islam during the long period of Ottoman rule.

Because of Adjaria's adherence to Islam, neighboring Turkey retains a strong interest in developments in the region.

Soviet troops and an armored vehicle patrolling the streets prior to the breakup of the Soviet Union in 1991.

Adjaria did not become a part of the Russian Empire until as late as 1878, and it was granted autonomy by Soviet Russia as part of an agreement with Muslim Turkey in 1921. Following the breakup of the Soviet Union, many Christian Georgians regarded Muslim Adjaria's autonomy as a threat to a unified Georgian nation. Tensions escalated in 1991 when Georgia's first president, Zviad Gamsakhurdia, announced his intention to end Adjaria's autonomous status. Mass demonstrations took place in Batumi, and when elections were held in 1991, parties in favor of Adjarian autonomy swept the board.

Since 1991 Aslan Abishidze has led Adjaria's local government and run the region virtually as a personal fiefdom. Tbilisi has effectively lost administrative control of Adjaria, although the Adjarian leadership has made it clear that it wishes to remain part of Georgia. Eduard Shevardnadze has since attempted to appease the Adjarians and has praised them as a model of stability in a turbulent part of the world.

Following the Rose Revolution a major crisis arose when the new Saakashvili government sought to restore central authority over Adjaria. Foreign governments and international organizations appealed to both sides to exercise restraint and resolve their differences peacefully. Abishidze resigned as leader of Adjaria on May 5, 2004.

Economically Adjaria has proven to be one of Georgia's most successful regions. The Adjarians have not been affected by the conflicts that have disrupted so much of Georgian life, and cross-border trade with fellow Muslims in Turkey is flourishing.

RELATIONS WITH RUSSIA

Despite early conflicts of interest, Russia and Georgia have developed constructive relations based on shared goals. Both countries would like to see their mutual border secure and the secessionist conflicts in Abkhazia, Ossetia, and Chechnya brought to a lasting settlement.

Following the breakup of the Soviet Union, Russia has been keen to maintain an influence in the Caucasus region. Georgia has made various concessions to Russia by joining the Commonwealth of Independent States (CIS) in 1993, and signing an agreement in 1995 that allowed Russia to retain four military bases and up to 20,000 troops in Georgia. These troops are employed mainly in peacekeeping roles in South Ossetia and on the Abkhazian border. In return Georgia has gained economic aid and Russian mediation in helping to resolve the conflict in South Ossetia.

A 1999 agreement called for Russia to close two of the military bases in 2001, and a new agreement in 2005 called for the withdrawal of the remaining two: the 62nd Base in Akhalkalaki (withdrawn in July 2007) and the 12th in Batumi (to be withdrawn by the end of 2008). In December 2006 tension continued over Russia's expressed support for Abkhazian and Ossetian separatists.

ECONOMY

UNDER COMMUNISM, Georgians enjoyed a higher standard of living than most people in the Soviet Union, mainly because of the country's tourism industry and variety of agricultural produce. In 1990 the Georgian economy was seriously weakened by the conflicts in the autonomous regions of Abkhazia and South Ossetia, where many lives were lost and valuable time and energy were wasted. In Abkhazia economic activity has virtually ceased; half the population has fled the country and many buildings lie in ruins. This is a tragedy for an area that, during the Soviet period, was one of the wealthiest in the Soviet Union. However, the autonomous region of Adjaria has for the most part avoided conflict and continues to flourish, especially in cross-border trade with Turkey and Armenia. By the end of 1996 Georgia's economy had shrunk to around one-third of its size in 1989. In an attempt to stabilize the economy, the International Monetary Fund and World Bank provided financial aid and advice. Georgia has made substantial economic gains since 2001, achieving positive gross domestic product (GDP) growth and curtailing inflation.

Now the largest share of Georgia's GDP is produced by agriculture, followed by trade, manufacturing, and transportation. Georgia's main exports are metals and ores, wine, nuts, and aircraft. The Georgian government is also making progress in reforming the tax code, enforcing taxes, and cracking down on corruption. In its report *Doing Business 2007* the World Bank praised Georgia's economic reforms. The country's GDP growth of 10 percent in 2006 was one of the highest in Europe.

Above: **A worker pushes a wheelbarrow along a gas power station in Gardabani. Developments in energy sources such as these help boost Georgia's economy.**

Opposite: **A farmer harvests grapes in the village of Akhasheni, located nearly 75 miles (120 km) east of Tbilisi. Georgian wine is little known in the West, despite being regarded as the best in the former Soviet Union, and having a tradition stretching back more than 2,000 years.**

FROM PUBLIC TO PRIVATE OWNERSHIP

Under the Soviet system, the Georgian economy was run on socialist principles—public ownership of the means of production (farms, offices, factories, and industry) coupled with a centralized, state-planned economy. In 1994 the government began a campaign of mass privatization, followed in 1996 by legislation that allowed for the private ownership of land and regulations for the operation of commercial banks. During the Soviet era the government fixed prices of essential goods and services. Today the costs of food, gas, electricity, transportation, and communications are controlled by market forces and are on a par with world levels.

Lining up for bread in Tbilisi. Georgia has been experiencing debt and inflation in recent years.

Georgia's new economic opportunities and the emerging private sector have led to a widening gap between a small, rich elite and the majority, whose material conditions have steadily worsened.

AGRICULTURE

Approximately 12 percent of the land in Georgia is used for agriculture. Under the Soviet system the traditional, small family farms and estates of the Georgian nobility were replaced by government-run collective farms that required many workers. Since 1996 most of these farms have been privatized and divided into smaller units for private ownership.

Garden plots have traditionally been popular in Georgia. Under the Soviet system they were viewed as valuable sources of extra income for their owners. During the Soviet period, according to some estimates, as much as 40 percent of Georgia's entire agricultural output was provided by produce from private plots.

TRADING

Georgia trades mainly with other former Soviet republics. Its main exports of grapes and other fruits, vegetables, wheat, barley, wine, brandy, vodka, livestock, light industry, machinery and metalworking equipment, chemicals, metallurgical products, and building materials go to:

Russia	17.8 percent	Bulgaria	4.9 percent
Turkey	14.1 percent	Armenia	4.6 percent
Azerbaijan	9.6 percent	Ukraine	4.4 percent
Turkmenistan	8.7 percent	Others	35.9 percent

Georgia's main imports of mineral fuels, food products, beverages, transportation equipment, chemicals, electrical machinery and equipment come from:

Russia	15.4 percent	Germany	8.3 percent
Turkey	11.4 percent	United States	5.9 percent
Azerbaijan	9.4 percent	Turkmenistan	3.8 percent
Ukraine	8.8 percent	Others	37 percent

In the countryside, many families farm their land without the benefit of modern equiptment.

The country's exceptionally sunny climate promotes the growing of subtropical crops. Tea and citrus fruits are grown in Adjaria, Guria, Samegrelo, Imereti, and Abkhazia. Wine grapes, tobacco, olives, figs, almonds, apples, pears, and some grains and sugar beets are also grown throughout western Georgia. Reclamation of swampy lowlands around the mouth of the Rioni River added fertile land for the production of tea, citrus fruit, grapes, tobacco, and silk.

The Alazani Valley in Kakheti is recognized as the country's premier winemaking region. Before 1991 Georgia was the leading producer of table wines in the Soviet Union. Plants such as geraniums, roses, jasmine, and basil thrive here and are used by the perfume industry.

In the highland areas and on the Kartalinian Plain, the climate favors crops such as barley, oats, apples, plums, and cherries, as well as sheep grazing. Mountainous areas such as Upper Svaneti are used mainly for sheep and goat farming. Nearly one-third of the working population is employed in the agricultural industry, making it the largest employer in the country. Combined with forestry, agriculture accounts for 17 percent of Georgia's GDP.

MINERAL WEALTH

Georgia is rich in nonferrous metals, including copper, lead, zinc, and some deposits of silver and gold. There are about 300 known mineral

OIL—THE GREAT GEO-ECONOMIC GAME

Georgia has little oil itself, but it has transportation and storage facilities that are used to move oil from neighboring Azerbaijan. Azerbaijan extracts oil from the Caspian Sea basin, one of the richest sources of oil in the Caspian Sea basin today. Many American and British oil companies have invested in the oil fields of the Caspian Sea basin. Georgia recently signed an agreement to expand a pipeline that links Azerbaijan with the Black Sea port of Batumi, which has one oil refinery. From Batumi the oil is transported by sea to Western markets.

Plans are afoot to extend the pipeline farther east to carry oil from Turkmenistan and Kazakhstan, both of which are oil-producing countries. The link may eventually be extended westward to Turkey, providing quick access to the Mediterranean Sea and then to Europe and the rest of the world. Such an arrangement would provide Georgia with a ready supply of petroleum, as well as a vital and profitable interest in the region's most important economic asset.

However, Georgia's plans to provide a link between Europe and the oil-producing countries of Central Asia conflict directly with Russia's interests. The Russians have their own pipelines running from Azerbaijan and Kazakhstan through southern Russia to the Black Sea port of Novorossisk. As a major force in the region, the Russians expect to have a say in the major economic assets of former Soviet republics. They also resent Western interference. A compromise was reached in 1995; as a result two pipelines will carry oil westward—one through southern Russia and the other through Georgia. Construction of the Baku–Tbilisi–Ceyhan (BTC) oil pipeline began in September 2002. One of the biggest engineering projects of the decade since the fall of the Soviet Union, the pipeline transports crude petroleum 1,098 miles (1,768 km) from the Caspian Sea to the Mediterranean Sea. It passes through Baku in Azerbaijan and Tbilisi in Georgia to reach Ceyhan in Turkey. The BTC pipeline began operation in May 2006.

ores in the republic, of which only half are currently being exploited. There are substantial reserves of clay that can be used to make cement and other building products. Since antiquity Georgia has been famous for its metallurgy. The area around Kutaisi is rich in manganese deposits, a mineral used to make high-grade steel. Georgia's main industrial center is Rustavi, located 20 miles (32 km) southeast of Tbilisi. Rustavi is a typical industrial town with iron and steel mills and various chemical plants. Here laminated sheet iron and seamless pipe products are made.

Throughout Georgia factories produce diverse goods such as farm equipment, locomotives, and tea-gathering machines for the local tea industry.

The dam at the Inguri hydroelectric plant.

Since independence energy has become an expensive commodity in Georgia. Before 1991 Georgia had all its energy needs met by the other republics, but now it has to buy gas and electricity at the world market rate.

ENERGY

Georgia's mountainous territory has many fast-flowing rivers that provide a source of abundant energy. More than 200 hydroelectric dams have been built to tap the energy of the Rioni, Kura, and Inguri rivers. Nevertheless most of Georgia's energy is imported. The primary source of energy is natural gas, imported mainly from Turkmenistan. The country also imports most of its oil, although there is an estimated 27 million tons (24 million metric tons) of untapped oil in Georgia. The constructions on the Baku–Tbilisi–Ceyhan oil pipeline and the Baku–Tbilisi–Erzerum gas pipeline have brought much-needed investment and job opportunities to Georgia. The northwest mountains yield coal, reserves of which are estimated to be about 400 million tons (360 million metric tons). Under Soviet rule these deposits were not mined, because other forms of fuel could be obtained cheaply elsewhere. Exploiting these natural resources to reduce reliance on outside suppliers is one of the most urgent tasks Georgia faces today.

TRANSPORTATION

Georgia has 12,580 miles (20,247 km) of roads and 756 miles (1,612 km) of rail lines.

Three major roads cross the Great Caucasus to provide a link with Russia—the Georgian Military Highway links Tbilisi to Vladikavkaz, another highway links Kutaisi to Vladikavkaz, and the third one links Sukhumi to Cherkessk. Armenia, Azerbaijan, and Turkey are linked to Georgia by numerous roads.

Infrastructure has a crucial role to play in the economic development of the region. The country's roads and ports can provide a bridge for goods and services from the West via Turkey and the Black Sea to the new markets of the Caucasus and Asia. The ports of Batumi, Sukhumi, and Poti were busy import centers in the Soviet period, and may regain their influence as the region develops. In 2006 Russia severed all air, sea, land, and railroad links with Georgia, as well as postal service and visa issuance because of a spy scandal. The only legal land border crossing at Zemo Larsi was also closed, diverting traffic into the separatist regions outside of Georgia's control. These harsh measures have led Georgia to seek new markets for their products elsewhere.

Tbilisi subway station. The country's rugged terrain prevents rail lines from being built across the Caucasus. The main railway line runs along the Black Sea coast, linking Sochi in Russia to Sukhumi, then to Kutaisi, and east to Tbilisi and into Azerbaijan.

TOURISM

Before 1991 the Black Sea coastal resorts were popular vacation spots for people from all parts of the Soviet Union. Every summer Sukhumi, Batumi, Pitsunda, and Gagra would be swamped with people attracted to the warm sea, fine beaches, and sunny climate. The upland areas also offer skiing, climbing, and scenic walks in a fresh mountain climate.

Unfortunately political unrest and conflicts, especially in Abkhazia, have nearly destroyed the tourism industry. Georgia's beaches and rich cultural attractions have great potential to become a major foreign currency earner by attracting tourists from the West. In 1996 only 600 foreign tourists visited Georgia. In 2005, however, tourist arrivals numbered 560,000.

Georgia's new economic opportunities and the emerging private sector have led to a widening gap between a small, rich elite and the poorer majority, whose material conditions have steadily worsened.

ENVIRONMENT

NEARLY 40 PERCENT OF GEORGIA is forested, and almost 10 percent of these forests are virgin old growth. Surprisingly, long periods of battle with opposing forces have not devastated the landscape, though in the 1990s many forested areas were threatened by illegal logging. Since independence Georgia has taken steps to evaluate and solve its environmental problems. The country faces similar global threats, such as deforestation, air pollution, and waste issues.

DEFORESTATION

The economic downturn of the 1990s hit the Caucasus region hard. When Russia halted timber export to Georgia, the country turned to intensive deforestation to meet its needs. There was also illegal cutting of forest to

Left: **Deforested trees silhouetted in the twilight.**

Opposite: **The village of Kazbegi is surrounded by beautiful mountains and lush greenery.**

supplement scarce fuel resources. The population now consumes three times more firewood than it did 10 years ago. Georgia's forests and wildlife have suffered as a result. Such economic pressures have resulted in a significant reduction of endemic plant communities. Some are now rare or endangered, and a few have become extinct. These include the Georgian elm, the Transcaucasian poplar, and the Eldari pine. With deforestation some of the signature animals of the Caucasus regions have gone extinct or nearly so. Among these are the four species of wild goat, the Persian gazelle, the striped hyena, and the Caucasian leopard.

The striped hyena is increasingly at risk of becoming extinct.

WATER POLLUTION

Industrial development during the Soviet era contributed to the pollution of the Black Sea.

Conditions may have improved following the downturn in Georgia's economy in the years following independence. Still industrial and medical discharges continue to pollute the seas. Inadequate sewage treatment adds to the problem, as less than 20 percent of wastewater is treated before being released into the sea. In addition power shortages often prevent the effective delivery of drinking water to the population. An estimated 70 percent of surface water contains health-endangering bacteria. This may account for Georgia's high rate of intestinal disease.

Children playing at a freshwater fountain located in central Tbilisi.

AIR POLLUTION

Road traffic is the major source of air pollution in Georgia, followed by the energy sector and industry. Numerous hazardous sources of ionizing radiation, such as communications equipment containing radioactive strontium and cesium, have been discovered in areas formerly occupied by Russian forces. In 1986 a nuclear power plant exploded in Chernobyl, some 750 miles (1200 km) away, in Ukraine. Prevailing winds brought radiation across the Black Sea. Georgia has since documented an increase of up to 20 percent more cases of anemia, a condition in which there

There are many harmful effects of air pollution. Here, a piglet is born deformed due to the Chernobyl fallout.

is a deficiency of red cells or hemoglobin in the blood, resulting in pallor and weariness, in pregnant women. Primary endocrine system diseases, as well as cancer and related sicknesses, have also increased since the accident.

In the post Soviet years the Georgian government attributed little importance to the country's environmental problems. In 1993 the minister for protection of the environment resigned in protest of this inactivity. In January 1994 a new, interdepartmental environmental monitoring system was introduced by the Cabinet of Ministers to centralize separate programs under the direction of the Ministry of Protection of the Environment. The Green Party fought vigorously on environmental issues in the parliament in 1993.

The United Nations Economic Commission for Europe states that nearly 60 percent of the annual forest harvest is unrecorded fuelwood.

A group of people burns firewood to keep warm. The depletion of wood in Georgia is partly caused by the need to use logs as fuelwood.

GEORGIANS

MODERN GEORGIA IS AN ETHNICALLY DIVERSE country, and many Georgians trace their ancestry to traders, invaders, and refugees from neighboring lands that settled in Georgia over the years. Because the country is mountainous, its people are broken into many small, independent groups. A 1989 Soviet census listed 96 distinct nationalities in Georgia. According to the 2007 census, of the 4.6 million people in the country today, Georgians make up 83.8 percent, or 3.9 million people. The other major ethnic groups are the Azeri (6.5 percent), Armenians (5.7 percent), Russians (1.5 percent), and others (2.5 percent). Ossetians, Greeks, and Abkhazians also reside in the republic.

During the Soviet period there was a policy to gradually merge the many nationalities of the Soviet Union into the "Soviet person"—one who would practice socialist principles and put political ideology before national culture. The peoples of Georgia found this ideology unappealing and lost little of their national spirit, despite pressure from Moscow.

It is estimated that as many as 1 million people have left Georgia because of the political and economic hardships of the 1990s. There are large émigré communities of Georgians in Russia, and smaller communities in the United States, France, and Britain.

Left: **The Georgians dress much like people in other parts of Europe, although fewer designer clothes are sold. During the Soviet period, when drab garments were the norm, Georgians still wore their clothes with an elegance that expressed their flamboyance and zest for life.**

Opposite: **A Georgian grandmother and her granddaughters sitting in front of a wall of framed family photos.**

A Georgian woman sits with her dog in front of an old part of Mtckheta.

KARTVELIAN PEOPLES

Georgians distinguish three Kartvelian peoples—the Georgians, Mingrelians, and Svans. A fourth group, called Laz, lives almost exclusively in modern-day Turkey. The Kartvelian people share a common language, history, and culture. The origin of the Kartvelians as a people is not known, but they are probably the result of a fusion of aboriginal Caucasian peoples with immigrants from Asia Minor. Nowadays, when people refer to Georgians, they usually mean all Kartvelian peoples, including the Svans and Mingrelians.

GEORGIANS The Georgians call themselves Kartvelebi (kart-VE-le-bi) and their country Sakartvelo (sa-KART-ve-lo). These names are linked to the mythical demigod Kartlos (said to be a great-great-grandson of Moses), who is considered the "father" of all Georgians. In the Western world the country's name is mistakenly believed to have come from its patron saint, Saint George. In fact, the name *Georgia* originates from

"Gurj," the name given to the people of Georgia by the Arabs and Persians.

Physically Georgians resemble the peoples of the eastern Mediterranean, but they are generally taller, with athletic, wiry bodies and dark hair and eyes. They are an elegant and attractive people. The women especially have a reputation for being graceful and beautiful. When the Ottoman Turks ruled the country, Georgian women were often carried off to the harems of the sultans.

The Georgians are proud, passionate, and fiercely individualistic, retaining a strong sense of family. They are renowned fighters with strict codes of personal honor and a long tradition of chivalry. They are hospitable, welcoming guests and travelers. Friendship is highly prized and celebrated in the country's 12th-century national epic, *The Knight in the Panther's Skin*, written by Shota Rustaveli.

The people behave and carry themselves with dignity and what many observers consider a sense of royalty. According to an unofficial census conducted many years ago, as many as one in seven Georgians claimed to be of royal descent.

On the hills above Tbilisi is a statue of Kartlis Deda (KART-lis DE-da), or "Mother Georgia." In her left hand she holds a bowl of wine, and in her right, a sword. This statue symbolizes the Georgian character—welcoming toward friends but fierce toward enemies.

MINGRELIANS It is estimated that there are nearly 1 million Mingrelians in Georgia, the majority of whom lives in the region of Samegrelo, their traditional homeland in the Kolkhida lowlands. Some people consider the Mingrelians the most beautiful people of the Caucasus because of their fair skin, blond hair, and blue eyes—rarities in this part of the world. Tea production has made the Mingrelians one of the wealthiest peoples in Georgia.

A man walks with his cow in the region of Upper Svaneti.

SVANS There are approximately 80,000 Svans in Georgia who live mainly in the mountainous regions of Upper and Lower Svaneti. Throughout the Middle Ages, the Mongol invasions, and the Turkish and Persian incursions of the 16th and 17th centuries, the Svans found themselves cut off from the mainstream of Georgian cultural and social life, safe and isolated in their mountain fortresses. Consequently their dialect has much in common with older rather than modern forms of Georgian.

The character of the Svans is very much a product of their harsh, mountainous environment. They are a proud, independent, and hardy people used to a stoical existence with few of the comforts of modern civilization. Hunters and climbers are the most respected members of the community. Vendettas and blood feuds between communities and families continue to this day. However, the Svans, like all Georgians, are very hospitable toward guests and travelers. They are famous for their songs, which are a complex form of Georgian polyphonic singing, and their dances.

ADJARIANS

The people of the Adjarian Autonomous Republic are mainly ethnic Georgians, although the majority is made up of Muslims. This is a result of Ottoman Turkish rule from the 16th to 19th centuries. Many Adjarians still have close cultural and family ties with the bordering Turkish provinces.

ABKHAZIANS

There are approximately 70,000 Abkhazians in Georgia. Despite their small numbers, they are a visible minority because they inhabit their own republic, the Abkhazian Autonomous Republic, along the northwest coast of the Black Sea.

The origin of the Abkhazian people is shrouded in mystery, although they have been in Georgia for about 2,000 years. They are thought to be a proto-Georgian people who, in the 17th century, mixed with the Adige, a northern Caucasian tribe, and, in doing so, lost their Georgian-oriented culture.

The Abkhazians are ethnically a northern Caucasian people who are different from the Kartvelian, or southern Caucasian people. They are a mountain people who have traditionally lived as shepherds.

The people have their own government and language, Abkhaz. Russian is spoken as a second language. Few Abkhazians speak good Georgian, although many of those who live in the south of Abkhazia, near Samegrelo, speak Mingrelian, the dialect of that region. Most Abkhazians are Muslims.

Because of the movement of people from other parts of Georgia and Russia in the late 19th and early 20th centuries, the Abkhazians are a minority in their homeland, making up only 18 percent of the population of Abkhazia. It is because of this imbalance and their perceived decline that the Abkhazians campaigned and fought for independence from Georgia throughout the 1990s.

Abkhazians being evacuated from Abkhazia, a region of civil unrest.

EXILES IN CENTRAL ASIA

Religion and ethnicity have created considerable problems in Georgia. In 1944 Stalin had 144,000 Muslim Georgians from the southwest province of Meskheti transported forcibly to Uzbekistan in Central Asia, a fate suffered by many ethnic groups throughout the Soviet Union in the 1930s and 1940s. Although successive Soviet regimes have acknowledged that these people did not commit any crimes, they have not been allowed to return to their homelands. There are about 300,000 Turkish Meskhetians living in the Commonwealth of Independent States, of which 80,000 are in Azerbaijan. The rest are temporarily living in Russia, Uzbekistan, and Kazakhstan. As recently as 2004, only 50,000 of Turkish Meskhetians were seeking to return to their historic residences.

Today Meskheti is populated by Christian Georgians and Armenians from other parts of the country. The Georgian government has so far opposed the return of the exiled Meskhetian Muslims, fearful that an increase in the Muslim population will create further ethnic and religious tension in an already fragile region.

Jews make up a minority group in Georgia.

OSSETIANS

The 2002 census puts the population of Ossetians in Georgia (excluding the South Ossetian Autonomous Region) at 38,028. About 515,000 are in Russia. Only 70,000 live in the South Ossetian Autonomous Region. The Ossetians are an Iranian people and are thought to be descendants of the ancient Alans, who came to the region in the sixth century A.D. They are essentially a mountain people and most of them are Christians, though there is a sizable Muslim minority, differences that set them apart from the Georgians. Many Ossetians would like to withdraw from the Georgian republic and unite their region with North Ossetia. The Georgians, however, believe that South Ossetia is historically a part of Inner Kartli and so they resist any attempt at separation.

OTHER PEOPLES

Because of the constant movement of people and shifts of power throughout the history of the Caucasus, many other peoples from the surrounding region have settled in Georgia. There are 267,900 Armenians in the country. The Armenians are Christians and have their own language and alphabet. They are spread throughout the world, mainly because of historical persecution by the dominant Turkish and Arab Muslims in South and West Armenia. Tbilisi has a large Armenian population, as do the regions of Meskheti and Dzhavakheti.

There are approximately 305,500 Azerbaijanis in Georgia, the majority of whom live south of Tbilisi, in and around the towns of Bolnisi and Marneuli. Most speak Azerbaijani and are Muslims.

About 67,000 Russians have also settled in Georgia. There are about 100,000 Greeks in Georgia, living mainly in the western part of the country, and there are smaller numbers of Ukrainians, Jews, and Kurds.

Theater performers in long braids wearing their traditional costumes.

DRESS

Occasionally on festival days, during celebrations, or for the fun of it, the Georgians dress in their distinctive traditional costume. Men wear the *cherkeska* (CHER-kes-kah), a knee-length tunic worn with soft, high, leather boots, and a *burkah* (BUR-kah), or woolen cape, flung over their shoulders. Georgian men like to appear masculine, and often wear daggers for special occasions, as well as cartridge cases sewn on the chest of their tunics. In Svaneti and Kakheti cylindrical-shaped woolen caps are traditional. The women also wear *cherkeskas*, although theirs are usually longer than the men's and are decorated with etched silver chains and buckles. Many women in the rural areas wear headscarves, but this traditional headgear is losing its popularity in cities

LIFESTYLE

GEORGIANS ARE TRADITIONAL in their ways, and family and marriage form the cornerstone of society. This traditional lifestyle is reinforced by a strong sense of national identity. Unfortunately the economic realities of the 1990s have seriously affected people's standard of living. Unemployment has risen sharply, and food prices have reached astronomical levels. In 1993—one of the worst years for Georgia, both politically and economically—80 percent of the people were estimated to be living below the official poverty line, although things have improved since then. In 2005 the unemployment rate had been reduced to 13.8 percent and 2.02 million people are now in the workforce.

Left: **Georgian women knitting in a park.**

Opposite: **Georgians waiting for the bus.**

A group outing in a park. In Tbilisi, as in many other Georgian cities, most summer activities are held outdoors.

COUNTRY AND CITY LIFE

Life in the cities improved during the Soviet era, but mountain communities were generally left out of the technological advances made in the lowland areas. This led to a steady drift of people to the cities.

In the cities it is popular to take a walk after work. People are in the habit of strolling up and down the main thoroughfares in the evening, talking, laughing, and occasionally going into a café for a glass of wine, brandy, or coffee. This custom offers young Georgians the opportunity to meet one another. In Tbilisi the most popular place for taking an evening walk is the tree-lined Rustaveli Avenue. Around this street are Tbilisi's best cafés, restaurants, shops, cinemas, and theaters. Elsewhere there is always something going on—people buying and selling things, playing games or musical instruments, eating together, or just chatting.

In the villages most people work on the land. It is common for Georgians to have their own fruit or vegetable plots and, in some cases, even vineyards in their back garden. The people's lives are dominated by the changing seasons. For example, Kakheti is a hive of activity in October when grapes are harvested. The villagers celebrate the bounty by decorating the balconies of their houses with bunches of grapes, and every available basket and bucket is filled to the brim with grapes.

An elderly couple enjoying a relaxed lifestyle.

HIGH LIVING

Georgians regard the mountainous provinces of the Caucasus to be the heart and soul of their country. Many of their traditions are believed to have originated there—the lavish hospitality, codes of honor, and the importance placed on friendship.

The mountainous areas are thinly populated compared with the lowlands. The winter population of places such as Khevi and Mtiuleti is only about 7,000 people per region. The lifestyle there is pastoral and lacks the advantages of modern technology. People generally make their living as shepherds and by growing a few vegetables on the limited amount of fertile land. The weather is harsh during the winter months, and there are frequent landslides and road accidents. Along many mountain roads it is common to find small, cagelike structures that serve as memorials that mark the spot where someone was killed. Inside each memorial is a picture of the deceased, a bottle of wine, and some drinking glasses. This allows passing friends and relatives to stop and drink to the memory of their loved one.

Imeretian peasants welcome guests in traditional style.

HOSPITALITY

Hospitality, generosity, and friendship are the codes by which Georgians live. They are known for their uninhibited hospitality, accosting friends and even strangers regularly and inviting them into their homes for an impromptu drink, snack, or meal. Georgian hospitality often means that meals last for hours and consist of many courses, toasts, and lengthy arguments and discussions. Although Georgians love their wine, they consider it bad taste to get drunk. The measure of a man's masculinity is often equated with his ability to hold his drink.

TO YOUR HEALTH!

The Georgians love to celebrate, and they take great pride in their toasting. Toasts are always initiated by the *tamada* (TA-ma-da), or toastmaster. Once the *tamada* has proposed the toast and drunk, the other guests may follow. If a toast honors a particular person, the assembled guests drink to that person first, allowing the individual to respond with a final toast of thanks. Often a special or honored guest will be presented with a *khantsi* (KAN-tsi), a large goat's horn filled to the brim with wine, and asked to drain it all at once. Important toasts usually mean that the glass is drained in a single gulp as a sign of respect. The last toast will be in honor of the *tamada*, and to a safe journey home. As the Georgians would say, "*Gauma . . . jos!*" (ga-u-MA . . . jos), or "Cheers!"

A bride in a modern Georgian wedding.

FAMILY AND MARRIAGE

Traditionally it is the man's family who seeks a bride and initiates marriage negotiations. This is normally done through a female relative, who assesses the suitability of unmarried women in the locality. A "chance" meeting will then be arranged to give the man and woman an opportunity to see one another. If there is some attraction, they will meet again, after which the man or a member of his family will approach the woman's parents to ask for her hand in marriage. When the marriage proposal is accepted, the groom produces a gold ring to mark the engagement. The bride's family gives a dowry, although this is usually small.

Church wedding ceremonies were rare during the Soviet era, but the tradition was gradually revived with the demise of Communism and an increase in religious practice. The main wedding ceremony is a social rather than a religious event. First the groom goes to the bride's house in a ribbon-decked car, followed by a noisy, colorful convoy of his family members. Following this the couple goes to a registry office to register the marriage and exchange rings. A celebration at the groom's home follows, which includes dinner, toasts, singing, and dancing, and is attended by the couple's families.

A *tamada*, usually one of the groom's uncles, acts as master of ceremonies. That night the couple spends their first night together in their own bedroom in the groom's family house. Feasting usually continues for several days. The day after the wedding, the bride is traditionally taken to fetch water from the local spring, where she will have the opportunity to meet the womenfolk of her new neighborhood.

In the past rural Georgians generally married someone from their home area, often from the same village. As a result of the increased social mobility that came with being a part of the Soviet Union, marriages among people from different parts of Georgia and even across the Soviet Union became more common.

CENTENARIANS

Georgians, like other Caucasian people, are famous for their longevity. It is a medical phenomenon that has attracted wide interest and for which experts can offer no concrete explanation. The statistics tell the story—the republic claims 51 centenarians for every 100,000 inhabitants.

The centenarians do not just live a long time; they usually live full lives, working, relaxing, and enjoying themselves as young people do. Longevity is particularly prevalent in Abkhazia, which has a famous choir—Nartaa (NAR-ta)—made up wholly of men 70 to 130 years old. Nartaa is an amazing sight and performs throughout Georgia, entertaining locals and visitors alike.

Surprisingly the average life expectancy for men in Georgia is 73 years and for women 80 years—unremarkable figures compared with those of the rest of the world. So why are there so many centenarians? Although there is no sure explanation, some observers think it is the Georgians' healthy diet (vast amounts of yogurt, fresh vegetables, and dairy products), healthy mountain air, fresh spring water, beneficial effects of the superior local brandy, and the Georgian love of life.

MALE DOMINATION

Georgia is a male-oriented society where the birth of a baby boy is celebrated more than that of a girl. Boys are usually spoiled by their mothers, which contributes to their sense of superiority. Georgian male role models are traditional and often old-fashioned. The most admired men in Georgia are bandits, warriors, and horsemen from the country's eventful past, all of whom are remembered in popular songs and dances. Boys are often named after these popular figures. Such role models influence the men's attitudes and reinforce the image of the macho male. This image is further reflected in the traditional costumes worn by men on special occasions—they are usually decked out in *cherkeska* and carry a sword, dagger, and gun cartridges.

Male and female roles are very clearly defined, and gender equality is not an issue in Georgia as it is in Western countries. Although they are not an inhibited race, the Georgians do observe a strict code of sexual morality. The men treat women with great respect, but not necessarily as equals. For example, the men are unlikely to help with household chores such as washing or cooking, which they consider feminine tasks.

Georgian women are traditionally feminine in their behavior and are not likely to engage in masculine work or pastimes. They consider being a wife and mother an ideal life choice. In the cities more women are financially independent, but are likely to live with their families until they marry, as is the case with their male counterparts.

Men in national dress. Family ties, camaraderie, and friendship are of the highest importance to Georgian men.

Georgia can only guarantee free education for the first nine years of school, starting at the age of six. College education has to be self-financed.

EDUCATION

Education has always been important to Georgians, and centers of learning can be traced back as far as the time of the Colchians. For much of history the Georgian Church ran the schools, providing the country with an educated class.

Under the Soviet system all Georgians were guaranteed free preschool, primary, secondary, and higher education. As a result Georgia has one of the highest proportions of college graduates among former Soviet countries. There are 19 colleges in Georgia. Some specialize in teacher training and others in agricultural studies. Also included are a medical school, an art academy, a music conservatory, and a theater institute—all in Tbilisi. The University of Tbilisi is Georgia's largest institution of higher learning. It was founded in 1917 following the Russian Revolution. There are 20 other university-level establishments. Enrollment in Georgian universities in 2003 numbered about 155,500. In recent years English language courses are also offered in some 30 secondary schools and two universities.

BENDING THE RULES

In the past Georgians always found that the Communist system limited their natural exuberance and entrepreneurial spirit. They have a special term—*blate* (blatè)—for getting around rules and regulations. The word can be roughly translated to mean obtaining benefits or favors through personal influence instead of by merit or through official channels. In its mildest form, it means simple patronage, and in its more extreme form, it means outright extortion or fraud. Because of this Georgians have earned themselves a reputation for black-market trading, especially in Russia.

The spirit of *blate* has, unfortunately, manifested itself in a more ominous form since independence, with the rapid growth of criminal, Mafia-type organizations throughout Georgia.

WORK AND WELFARE

Georgians work normal office hours, although the shops are open from 8:00 A.M. to 9:00 P.M. on most days. The right to strike is recognized by the Georgian constitution. Allowances are given to the unemployed, single mothers, and refugees. However, the amount is so small—just a few dollars a month—that it does not provide an adequate welfare safety net.

All Georgians are entitled to basic health care. Georgia has a high-quality, state-run health system that includes 500 hospitals and more than 17,000 doctors. Unfortunately the government has had problems in recent years finding the money needed to operate the system effectively. Some hospitals are being privatized, offering people a choice of services.

Although welfare allowances are small and the government has limited resources, it is trying to direct attention to those most in need, especially the elderly.

RELIGION

GEORGIA IS A MULTIRELIGIOUS country where freedom of religious expression is guaranteed in the constitution. In Tbilisi, for example, there is a Jewish synagogue, a Muslim mosque, a Georgian basilica, an Armenian church, and a Zoroastrian temple, all within a 15-minute walk of one another.

Although there is no official state religion, the Georgian Orthodox Church is accorded special importance and is nominally supported by 83.9 percent of the population. Throughout history, and especially during the tsarist and Soviet eras, the Georgian Orthodox Church provided a powerful focus for the country's patriotism and nationalism.

The other main religions in the republic are Islam (9.9 percent), the Armenian Gregorian Church (3.9 percent), the Russian Orthodox Church (2 percent), and the Catholic Church (0.8 percent). Less than 1 percent declared themselves to be an adherent to other religions, while 0.7 percent declared no religion at all in the 2002 census.

Above: **A mosque located in South Ossetia.**

Opposite: **The Tasminda Sameba Church in Tbilisi.**

GEORGIAN ORTHODOX CHURCH

Christianity came to Georgia in A.D. 330. The story of the country's conversion is a mixture of fact and legend. Tradition says that a slave woman, who later came to be known as Saint Nino, cured the Iberian Queen Nana of a strange illness. This proved Nino's holiness and helped her gain the queen's confidence. Legend has it that the queen's husband, King Mirian, was converted when he found himself enveloped suddenly in pitch darkness while on a hunting trip. He then invoked the Christian God, and the light of day returned. It is thought that he actually saw an eclipse of the sun and mistook it for a divine event.

The Orthodox Church faces a new challenge to integrate itself into the more Westernized society promoted by President Saakashvili. In 2006 the Georgian Orthodox Church reported having 30 dioceses, 1,004 parish priests, and 65 monasteries.

In western Georgia Christianity replaced early beliefs that were based on a pantheon of Greek gods, and in eastern Georgia it replaced an Iranian Zoroastrian religion. The conversion to Christianity had a profound effect on Georgian culture and history. The country suddenly became one of the few Eastern outposts of Christianity with its cultural and social orientation toward Christian Europe, away from the Islamic civilizations to the south and east.

In the fifth century, the church became autonomous and appointed its own leader, the Catholicos of Mtskheta. Throughout the Middle Ages the Georgian Church held enormous political and economic power and inspired a tradition of art, architecture, and literature.

Under tsarist rule, however, the church lost its independence and was treated as a branch of its much larger brother, the Russian Orthodox Church. The independent status of the Georgian Church was reestablished during the Soviet era when Stalin—who had trained for the priesthood in Georgia—intervened on its behalf. Despite this, many of the 2,000 churches in Georgia were closed and left to deteriorate, and it is only over the last 20 years that the churches have been reopened and restoration work has begun.

PRACTICES The Georgian Orthodox Church is part of the Eastern branch of Christianity, the Orthodox Church. It is practiced in much of Eastern Europe and Greece. The Eastern churches split formally from Western Christianity in the 11th century, and do not recognize the Pope in Rome as their head, nor do they observe any of the Western Church's holy days. The Orthodox churches have never had a central body or leader, as the Catholic Church does. The current head of the Georgian Church is Catholicos Ilya II. Georgian Orthodox practice is similar to that of the other Orthodox churches, although it differs in some of its liturgical rules and rituals. Christmas and Easter are the most important days in the Georgian Orthodox calendar.

Orthodox practice has more in common with Catholic rather than Protestant practice. Ritual is important and includes music, the burning of incense, and chanting. Icons are positioned around the inside of most churches, and walls are covered with frescoes depicting religious events. Believers pray in front of the icons, lighting candles as offerings and often kissing the icons as a mark of devotion. Orthodox services are usually sung in Georgian. The combined experience is intended to convey the essence of Christianity, appealing to worshippers' emotional, intellectual, and aesthetic faculties.

Since the late 1980s there has been a revival of faith in Georgia, especially among the rural population. More children are being baptized, and church weddings are becoming popular. The government has encouraged the revival as a healthy expression of the national spirit.

Georgia's patron saint, Saint George, pictured slaying a dragon. Saint George's Day is celebrated on November 23.

SAINT GEORGE

Saint George is the patron saint of Georgia, and icons showing him slaying a dragon are often found in Georgian churches. In pagan times the worship of heroes and warriors was common. Saint George, as a strong and dashing warrior saint, was the ideal figure to fill this role after the country's conversion to Christianity, and he is revered even today.

The Cathedral of Sveti-tskhoveli in Mtskheta. The present cathedral dates from the 11th century and is the third building to be erected on the site.

CHURCH OF THE LIFE-GIVING PILLAR

The Cathedral of Sveti-tskhoveli in Mtskheta is one of the most sacred places in Georgia. The site was chosen for one of Georgia's first churches in the fourth century because it was the burial place of an early Georgian saint, Sidonia. A cedar tree grew from the grave, and King Mirian ordered seven columns to be made from its trunk to provide the church's foundations. It is said that when the sixth column was completed, the seventh rose magically by itself into the air and could only be put into place when Saint Nino interceded through prayer. It was also believed that a sacred liquid flowing from the column could cure all diseases. In Georgian the word *sveti* (SVE-ti) means "column," and *tskhoveli* (ts-KOV-el-i) means "life-giving."

RUSSIAN ORTHODOX CHURCH

Christianity reached Georgia before it reached Russia; the Georgian Orthodox Church is older than the much larger Russian Orthodox Church by about six centuries.

In Georgia only 2 percent of the people are Russian Orthodox Christians. Russian Orthodoxy originated from Kievan Rus (the kingdom of Rus, originally centered around Kiev) in the 10th century when Christianity first arrived there. Over the next few centuries it became the religion of all Russians. In the 19th century Russian and Ukrainian migrants brought it to Georgia from tsarist Russia. The tsarist authorities encouraged the establishment of monasteries in an attempt to strengthen their influence in the region as part of their Russification policy. One of the most famous of these is Novy Afon (New Athos), built in Abkhazia in 1900. Russian churches are found mainly along the coast of the Black Sea and in larger cities such as Tbilisi and Kutaisi.

The Russian Orthodox Church is the largest Eastern church and is the chief representative of the precepts of Orthodoxy. The head of the church is the Patriarch of All Russia.

The unusual shape of the Georgian cross is ascribed to Saint Nino. It is said that upon entering Georgia, she took two vine branches and tied them into a cross using strands from her own hair, thus producing an imperfectly shaped cross.

ARMENIAN APOSTOLIC CHURCH

The Armenian Apostolic Church is marginally older than the Georgian Orthodox Church, and was founded in the late third century by Gregory the Illuminator. In converting the Armenian king (King Tiridates III), Gregory, in effect, created the world's first truly Christian state. The Armenian Church separated from the other Eastern churches in the sixth century and is still autonomous today. It is headed by the Catholicos of Echmiadzin near Yerevan, Armenia.

A fresco in a church. The Armenian Church differs in dogma and practice from both the Georgian Orthodox Church and mainstream Orthodoxy.

Armenian churches tend to have simple decorations. They practice the custom of hanging ostrich eggs from the ceilings of the churches as symbols of hope and resurrection. Georgia contains the largest community of practicing Apostolic Armenians outside of Armenia. Armenians first began migrating to Georgia in the 14th and 15th centuries as a result of persecution by the Muslim Turks and Arabs.

ISLAM

Islam is a major religion in the Caucasus—many of the peoples in the Russian regions north of Georgia are Muslim, as are the populations of Turkey and Azerbaijan. Georgia has historically been perched on the northern edge of the Islamic world, and the Islamic religion has left its mark on the republic. Georgia's Azerbaijani population consists of Azerbaijians, as well as the Abkhazians, Ossetians, and most of the ethnic Georgians in Adjaria.

JUDAISM

There have been Jewish communities in Georgia since the Middle Ages. The largest Jewish communities are found in Kutaisi and Tbilisi; smaller groups can be found in the mountain regions. At one time 2 percent of the population of Kutaisi was Jewish, although over the last 20 years, the Jewish presence has been reduced significantly by massive emigration to Israel. There are fewer than 8,000 Jews in Georgia today.

A place of worship for the Jewish community living in Georgia.

ᲙᲕᲘᲚᲘ
5 ᲘᲐᲜᲕᲐᲠᲘ — ᲐᲠᲩᲔᲕᲜᲘᲗᲘ. ᲠᲝᲛᲔᲚᲗᲐᲗᲕ
ᲡᲐᲥᲐᲠᲗᲕᲔᲚᲝᲡ ᲣᲜᲓᲐ ᲨᲔᲣᲠᲩᲔᲚᲝᲗ

LANGUAGE

WITHIN THE SMALL AREA of the Caucasus there is an enormous variety of languages. Consequently many different languages are spoken in Georgia. The Roman writer Pliny recorded in the first century A.D. that the Romans needed 130 different interpreters to do business in the Caucasus. Strabo, the ancient Greek geographer, recorded in the same period that as many as 70 different languages were spoken daily in the market in Dioscuris (modern-day Sukhumi).

Georgian is the most widely spoken of the Caucasian languages. It is the official language of the Georgian republic and is spoken as a first language by approximately 71 percent of Georgia's population. Other local languages are spoken domestically in the various regions of the nation.

Above: **The durability of the Georgian language has probably contributed more than any other factor to the survival of Georgian culture and the Georgians as a people.**

Opposite: **A man reads the newspaper while his friend peers over.**

GEORGIAN

Georgian belongs to the Kartvelian (South Caucasian) family of languages, which also includes Mingrelian, Laz, and the archaic Svan. All of these languages originated from Old Kartvelian (circa 2000 B.C.). Georgian does not fit into any of the major European language groups; despite numerous attempts, no one has managed to establish a relationship between Georgian and any other language or language family, even within the Caucasus. The Caucasian languages are grouped together for geographical convenience rather than linguistic similarity.

Of the more than 70 Caucasian peoples—excluding the Armenians—only the Georgians had a written language of their own before Russian colonization in the 19th century. Because of Georgia's turbulent history, the Greco-Roman, Persian, Arabic, Turkish, and, most recently, Russian, languages have all left their mark on the Georgian language.

Russian was the only compulsory language taught in Georgian schools during the Soviet era. Following independence, however, learning Georgian has become compulsory for all Georgians, and all of the main curriculum subjects in schools are taught in Georgian.

REGIONAL DIALECTS The Georgian literary standard is based on the language of the Kartli region around the capital, Tbilisi. However, Georgian includes a number of regional dialects: Imeruli (spoken in Imereti), Rachuli (spoken in Racha), Guruli (spoken in Guria), Khaxuri (spoken in Kakheti), and Acharuli (spoken in Adjaria). Minor dialects such as Psavuri, Xevsuruli, Tusuri, and Mtiulur-Gudamaqruli are also spoken in the remote mountain regions of Pyavi, Khevsureti, Tusheti, and Mtiuleti, respectively.

Fruit vendors speaking to their customers in the Tbilisi Central Market. Many of these vendors are fluent in Georgia's multiple dialects.

HISTORY OF THE GEORGIAN LANGUAGE

The Georgian alphabet was originally developed to aid the spread of Christianity. Christianity became the official religion of Iberia (modern-day Kartli and Kakheti) and Armenia in the fourth century A.D. The Iberians used Greek and Syriac texts for worship, but soon found a pressing need for a vernacular language to spread the new religion. A commission was set up to produce an alphabet that would represent the sounds of the Georgian and Armenian languages. In the fifth century a system of writing based on the Greek alphabet was developed. The oldest Georgian inscriptions that have been discovered date from A.D. 430 and were found in a church near Bethlehem in Israel.

Georgian texts have traditionally been grouped into one of three periods: old Georgian (fifth to 11th centuries), medieval Georgian (12th to 18th centuries), and modern Georgian (18th century to the present). Medieval Georgian reached its zenith in the periods of David the Builder and Queen Tamar, especially in the work of Georgia's greatest lyrical poet, Shota Rustaveli.

Shota Rustaveli, in a portrait from a manuscript in the State of Art Museum of Georgia, created in the 12th or 13th century.

Georgia only began to recover from the ravages of the Mongol conquest in the 18th century, and a unified literary language developed and flourished in the 19th century. Ilya Chavchavadze (1837–1907), the famous writer, did the most to modernize and promote the developing Georgian literary language. During the same period Jacob Gogebashvili (1840–1912) wrote *The Georgian Alphabet* (1865) and the definitive book on the Georgian language, *Native Speech* (1876).

Under the Soviet system Georgian was recognized as a state language of one of the Soviet Union's constituent republics and was consequently allowed to flourish with institutional support.

THE GEORGIAN ALPHABET

Since its adaptation into a written form, the Georgian language has progressed through three alphabet systems. The one used today is called Mxedruli (m-ked-RU-li), meaning "secular writing." It is so called because in the 11th century it replaced a script called "church writing." The spelling for Mxedruli script is straightforward: Each letter has its own pronunciation, and each sound always corresponds to the same letter.There are no long vowel sounds in Georgian.

There are 33 letters in the modern Georgian alphabet, including five vowels and 28 consonants. There is no distinction between upper- and lowercase letters. Like most languages, Georgian is written from left to right.

One of the many signboards featuring the Georgian script.

PRONUNCIATION GUIDE

Mxedruli script (m-ked-RU-li)	Mxedruli script transliteration	Simplified English pronunciation
ა	*a*	similar to the short *a* in *hat*
ბ	*b*	pronounced as the English *b*
გ	*g*	pronounced as the English *g*
დ	*d*	pronounced as the English *d*
ე	*e*	similar to the short *e* in *pet*
ვ	*v*	pronounced as the English *v*
ზ	*z*	pronounced as the English *z*
თ	*t*	pronounced as the English *t*
ი	*i*	similar to the short *i* in *hit*
კ	*k'*	pronounced as the English *k*, but glottalized
ლ	*l*	pronounced as the English *l*
მ	*m*	pronounced as the English *m*
ნ	*n*	pronounced as the English *n*
ო	*o*	similar to the short *o* in *hot*
პ	*p'*	pronounced as the English *p*, but glottalized
ჟ	*zh*	pronounced as the letters *si* in *vision*
რ	*r*	similar to a rolled *r*
ს	*s*	similar to a soft *s*, as in *hiss*
ტ	*t'*	pronounced as the English *t*, but glottalized
უ	*u*	similar to *oo*, as in *hook*
ფ	*p*	similar to the *p* in *pot*
ქ	*k*	similar to the *k* in *kit*
ღ	*gh*	similar to the *ch* in *porch*, but pronounced with a vibration
ყ	*q'*	similar to the English *k*
შ	*sh*	similar to the *sh* in *shirt*
ჩ	*ch*	similar to the *ch* in *church*
ც	*ts*	similar to the *ts* in *pits*
ძ	*dz*	similar to the *dz* in *adze*
წ	*c'*	similar to the *ts* in *pits*, but glottalized
ჭ	*ch*	pronounced as the *ch* in *church*, but glottalized
ხ	*kh*	similar to the *ch* in *porch*
ჯ	*j*	similar to the *dge* in *edge*
ჰ	*h*	pronounced as the English *h*

Women chatting together at a cafe.

LEARNING GEORGIAN

Georgian (also known as Kartuli) is a complex language that is difficult to learn. It contains a complex set of rules that govern verbs, as well as many formidable clusters of consonants—for example, *Tbilisi* (t-BLI-si)—that can baffle and frustrate the foreign student. Other examples are *trtvili* (TR-t-vi-li), meaning "frost," and *brtskinvale* (br-ts-kin-VA-le), meaning "brilliant." Georgian also includes many glottal stops, similar to the sound that English Cockneys make when they say "bottle" (BOH-ul). Vowels are short and sharp, and the people roll their *R*s.

Fortunately all 33 Georgian letters correspond to only one sound each, so confusion does not arise with them. Where there are two or three syllables in a word, the stress usually falls on the first syllable. For words with four or more syllables, the situation is more complicated.

OTHER TONGUES

There are many ethnic groups in Georgia and just as many languages that are spoken as either a first or second language.

MINGRELIAN, LAZ, AND SVAN These belong to the Kartvelian group of languages. Mingrelian is spoken along the central and southern coastal areas of the Black Sea, mainly in Samegrelo. Laz is spoken mainly in parts of Georgia close to northeastern Turkey. Mingrelian and Laz were originally subdivisions of the ancient Colchian tongue.

DIVIDED BY MANY TONGUES

Language	Spoken as a first language	Spoken as a second language
Georgian (including Mingrelian)	3,900,000	270,000
Russian	340,000	1,700,000
Ossetian	130,000	—
Armenian	370,000	—
Azerbaijani	300,000	—
Abkhazian	92,000	—
Svan	30,000	—

Svan has no alphabet, and is spoken mainly at home and socially by the people of the small mountain communities of Svaneti. Svan has preserved more of old Kartvelian than Georgian, probably because of the isolation of the Svans at various times throughout history.

In the 1930s the Mingrelian and Svan people were classified collectively as Georgians, and their languages were categorized as Georgian dialects. Since then the Mingrelians and Svans have received their education in Georgian and are classified as Georgian speakers.

ABKHAZIAN There are about 90,000 speakers of Abkhazian in the Abkhazian Autonomous Republic. The Georgian constitution recognizes this as the state language of Abkhazia. Abkhazian is a member of the small northwest Caucasian family of languages that includes Circassian and the almost extinct Ubykh, which is still spoken in parts of Turkey.

Abkhazian is not related to the Georgian language, and many Abkhazians speak poor Georgian, preferring instead to use Russian as their second language. The first Abkhazian alphabet was devised in 1862, but a wide selection of publications in Abkhazian became common only during the Soviet period. Television programs have been broadcast in Abkhazian since 1978.

OSSETIAN, AZERBAIJANI, AND ARMENIAN Ossetian, the language of ethnic Ossetians, is spoken in various parts of Georgia, especially in South Ossetia. It is part of the Iranian group of languages. Azerbaijani and Armenian, the national languages of Georgia's two neighbors, are spoken by Azerbaijanis and Armenians living in Georgia.

RUSSIAN As the language of the Soviet Union and of the tsarist authorities who ruled prior to the 1917 Russian Revolution, Russian has been spoken in Georgia for 200 years. Today it is still a popular language for those communities—such as the Ossetians, Abkhazians, Armenians, and Azerbaijanis—who do not speak Georgian well.

NAMES

As can be expected in a country with many ethnic groups, Georgians are named according to their ethnic and linguistic background. Members of Georgia's Muslim population—made up of the Azerbaijanis, Ossetians, and Abkhazians—often take traditional Islamic names, while Russians and Armenians use names from their own languages.

Popular Georgian men's names include Georgi, Nerab, Shota, David, Pavele, Alec, and Soso. Popular female names include Marina, Tamara, Lamara, Tamriko, Tsitsi, Thea, Lili, and the ubiquitous Mary.

Many Georgian surnames end in *-idze* or *-adze* (meaning "son of"), or *-vili* (meaning "child").

PUBLICATIONS, RADIO, AND TELEVISION

For a country with a long literary tradition, it is not surprising that Georgia has many newspapers and periodicals. Since the glasnost period of the late 1980s and subsequent independence, a steady number of new periodicals and newspapers has been published.

There are about 150 newspapers published in Georgia, of which 120 are written in Georgian. The principal newspapers in Georgian are *Young*

This Georgian baby may grow up speaking many languages, for there is no lack of media communication to cater to the needs of the various communities in Georgia.

Iberian, *Literary Georgia*, *Native Land*, *Free Georgia*, *Georgian Herald*, and *Republic of Georgia*. There are also newspapers published in Russian, Armenian, Abkhazian, and Ossetian. Of the 75 magazines in Georgia, 60 are written in Georgian.

Georgia's national radio and television networks are government-owned and government-controlled. Radio shows are broadcast in Georgian, Russian, Armenian, Azerbaijani, and English, while television programs are shown in Georgian and Russian.

COMMUNICATIONS

The telecommunications system in Tbilisi was upgraded in 1998, and further improvements to the system in the rest of the country were completed in two years. About 20 percent of the urban population now has telephone main lines. In rural areas there are about four telephones per 100 people. Nationwide pager service is available. Tbilisi, Kutaisi, and Batumi have cellular telephone networks for their 1.7 million mobile telephone users.

There are at least 10 Internet service providers that cater to 332,000 users in Georgia. However, broadband and e-commerce are yet to be developed in this country.

ARTS

GEORGIA HAS A RICH ARTISTIC HERITAGE stretching as far back as the second millennium B.C. It has been able to absorb the artistic influences of neighboring Turkey, the Middle East, and Russia, while retaining a style and an expression that are strictly Georgian. In Georgia art has rarely been used as a vehicle for social change, but it has provided the fiercely independent Georgians with a means of expressing their national character and affirming their cultural independence.

Above: **Woven carpets and rugs are some of the crafts found in Georgia.**

Opposite: **The Circle of Statues found in Tbilisi.**

METALWORK

The Georgians were fabled in the ancient world for their skill at metallurgy. Finds in tombs at Trialeti show that the Bronze Age Georgians were highly accomplished at smelting, forging, soldering, and embossing items with a high level of precision. In the fourth and fifth centuries, Georgian jewelry was second to none in the ancient world.

Following Georgia's conversion to Christianity, iconography and book illumination—a technique where handwritten books were illustrated or decorated as an art form—became popular from the eighth century A.D., and represent some of the world's earliest examples of the medieval goldsmiths' skill. The 10th-century Ishkani Processional Cross and Khobi Icon of the Virgin Mary, and the 11th-century Martvili Cross and silver roundel of Saint Mamai from Gelati are some of the beautiful pieces that can be seen in the Georgian State Museum in Tbilisi. The most famous piece in the museum is the 10th-century Khakhuli Triptych, which is embossed with rubies, pearls, and enamel. The Triptych is a masterpiece of medieval craftsmanship and was believed to have miraculous powers.

Some buildings found in Tbilisi's Arab quarter.

ARCHITECTURE

Georgians appear to have an affinity for stone, and their architecture combines the practical with the picturesque. There are many cathedrals, churches, monasteries, castles, and fortifications throughout Georgia.

The most popular style of dwelling is the rustic house known as *darbazi* (dar-BA-zi), which dates back to ancient times. The center of the darbazi tapers into a pyramid made from wooden logs, with successive layers piling up to form a chimney at the top. Modern variations of these can be found in central Georgia, usually decorated with beautifully carved doors, lintels, and fireplaces.

CHURCH ARCHITECTURE Georgian religious architecture thrived in the golden age of King David the Builder and Queen Tamar. Two designs for churches were popular: the domed type and the basilica. Domed churches have either a square or hexagonal-shaped central section. Basilica churches have a large rectangular center with aisles on each side.

Variations of the domed church first appeared in Georgia in the sixth and seventh centuries. The most famous of these is the Church of Dzhvari, which is spectacularly situated on a cliff at the confluence of the Aragvi and Kura rivers, a few miles from Tbilisi. The famous Cathedral of Svetitskhoveli (Church of the Life-Giving Pillar) can be found at Mtskheta. It is a basilica-type church built in the 11th century. The arcaded interior walls are covered with grotesque beasts carved in stone. The story of the building of this church is told in Constantine Gamsakhurdia's historical novel, *The Hand of the Great Master*.

The Bagrat Cathedral located in Kutaisi.

The Alaverdi Cathedral in Kakheti and Bagrat Cathedral at Kutaisi also date from the 11th century. King David the Builder founded the well-known Gelati Monastery in 1106. The monastery complex consists of three churches, an academy building, and the tomb of the king, who had also intended the monastery to be a center of learning. The development of religious architecture came to an end with the Mongol invasion in the 13th century.

FORTRESSES AND CAVE TOWNS Because of the many conflicts fought on Georgian soil, it is impossible to travel very far in the republic without coming across a fortress or castle. Situated on the Solalaki Ridge and dominating the skyline above the old section of Tbilisi are the ruins of the massive Narikala Fortress. Arab lords built the towers and walls in the eighth century on the site of fortifications that had been erected by King Vakhtang Gorgasali. The strategic importance of this fortress was such that King David the Builder—and after him, the Mongols, Turks, and Persians—all rebuilt and extended the fortifications, making it a hybrid of styles. Part of the fortress was destroyed when gunpowder that was being stored there was struck by lightning in 1827.

Ananuri is a superb 16th-century fortress complex situated near the Georgian Military Highway, 40 miles (64 km) north of Tbilisi. Its crenellated

A view of the Vardzia Caves, showing a town of cave dwellings carved within the mountains.

walls and defensive towers make it one of the more memorable monuments along the highway. The dukes of Aragvi, a violent feudal family, built the fortress as a residence and sanctuary during their frequent feuds with rival dukes.

Georgia has some very impressive cave architecture, rivaled only by similar dwellings in the Middle East. Uplis-Tsikhe, south of Gori in Kartli, is a city made of caves carved into the soft stone of the cliffs and hills that overlook the Kura River. It grew over a period of hundreds of years in the first millennium B.C. The city continued to flourish throughout antiquity, and was an important trading center in the Middle Ages, with a population of 20,000. It was sacked by the Mongols in the 13th century and never regained its former importance. The weather has slowly eroded the cave city, although the shapes of the dwellings and the city walls are still visible.

The caves were used as a place of worship; an impressive church basilica dates from the ninth century. Uplis-Tsikhe served as a prototype for the cave monasteries that developed later at David-Garedzha and Vardzia. David-Garedzha is a complex of 12 monasteries built amid the semilunar landscape of the Garedzha Hills in Kakheti, a few miles from the Azerbaijan border.

THE VARDZIA CAVES The Vardzia Caves, spectacularly situated 10,000 feet (3,048 m) above sea level in the Lesser Caucasus, form a vast complex of man-made cave dwellings, palaces, churches, and monasteries.

The caves are carved out of soft tufa and were first used as secular dwellings in the fifth century B.C. A Christian religious community expanded them in the eighth and ninth centuries A.D., and Queen Tamar used the caves to create a monastery and a center of Georgian culture in the late 12th century.

The Vardzia Caves represent the apex of cave architecture and a supreme expression of the Georgian religious spirit. Some of the 500 or so individual cave dwellings have their own small churches. The centerpiece of the complex is the Church of the Assumption, carved out of the cliff in 1184 on the instructions of Queen Tamar. The church contains many magnificent frescoes as well as inscriptions and portraits dedicated to the queen and her father, King Giorgi III. The most monumental religious fresco depicts the Virgin and Child. Other frescoes on religious themes include portrayals of the crucifixion, Jesus's descent into hell, and the raising of Lazarus from the dead.

Upper Svaneti's stone watchtowers served as homes as well as a military fort.

WATCHTOWERS OF UPPER SVANETI

In the remote mountain region of Upper Svaneti, many traditional peasant houses have an unusual feature: a 90-foot (27-m) stone tower. The earliest towers date from the 12th century. Although built as a defensive structure that allowed the Svans to see their enemies approaching from a distance, the size of a tower also indicated the power and standing of a family within the community. Each tower traditionally had four floors—the first for storing fodder and livestock, the second for religious devotions, and the third and fourth for the family and garrison. The towers are remarkably sturdy and have withstood landslides and avalanches that have swept away many newer buildings. It is thought that they were so strong because egg yolk was used in the mortar.

King Vakhtang VI supported literature in the early 18th century.

RUSSIAN INFLUENCES Because of the tsarist Russification policy, Russia's neoclassical style imposed itself on Georgia in the 19th century. However, the Russians' strict notions of classical order were subverted by the flamboyant charm of the Caucasus, so a hybrid style developed. Many of these hybrid buildings can still be seen in Tbilisi.

Many large, ugly municipal buildings sprang up under the Soviet regime. The only contemporary construction that is worthy of any mention is the building of the Ministry of Highways in Tbilisi, built in 1977. Paradoxically, Oriental styles from Georgia and other Central Asian Soviet republics influenced building styles in Soviet Russia as well.

LITERATURE

Georgia has an independent literary tradition that dates back to the fifth century A.D., when a distinctive Georgian alphabet came into being. The earliest works of Georgian literature were historical and religious, translating biblical and scriptural texts and describing the lives of Georgian saints. Jacob Tsurtaveli's *The Martyrdom of St. Shushanik* (476–83) is the earliest of these. The earliest Georgian chronicle, *The Conversion of Iberia*, written in the seventh century, describes the mission of Saint Nino. Georgian writing of this period was also influenced by contact with early Christian and Arabic literature, and many Persian tales were recast in Georgian form.

In Shota Rustaveli's (c. 1172–c. 1216) epic masterpiece, *The Knight in the Panther's Skin,* written in the late 12th to early 13th centuries, Georgian medieval literature reached its zenith. Written during Queen Tamar's illustrious reign, this long epic poem embodies the cultural sophistication of the period, and reflects the influence of Chinese, Persian, and ancient Greek philosophy. It has a universal appeal and has been translated into most major languages.

After the Mongol invasions of the 13th and 14th centuries, Georgian cultural and artistic life stagnated. Georgian literature eventually revived in the 16th century, renewing its ties with Muslim Oriental verse. In the early part of the 18th century, King Vakhtang VI (1675–1737), a poet and scholar, codified Georgia's laws in the Code of Vakhtang, and set up Georgia's first printing press.

Following Russian annexation, Prince Alexander Chavchavadze (1787–1846) and Grigol Orbeliani (1800–83) were the first representatives of a thriving Romantic movement among the Georgian aristocracy. In the 19th century many Georgian intellectuals studied in Russia and traveled throughout Europe, gaining greater exposure to new ideas. Despite heavy tsarist censorship, Georgian writers turned to social themes in the latter

ABKHAZIAN WRITING

Abkhazian literature came into being at the end of the 19th century. An Abkhazian alphabet was first created in 1862 and the first Abkhazian newspaper was printed in 1919. Dmitri Gulia (1874–1960) was a major promoter of Abkhazian writing and culture and founded Abkhazian prose with his short story, "Under Alien Skies," in 1919. Samson Chanba (1886–1937) wrote in both Abkhazian and Russian, and his plays drew on themes from revolutionary history. Fazil Iskander (b. 1929), a contemporary writer from Sukhumi, writes in Russian and is distinguished for his subtlety, humor, and philosophical character. His poetry collections and novella, *Kozlotur's Constellation*, have been widely read in Russian-speaking countries.

Ilya Chavchavadze did much to modernize and promote the Georgian literary scene in the late 19th century.

part of the 19th century, reflecting many of the political concerns that were current in Russia and Europe at the time. Two leading figures in this movement were the writers Ilya Chavchavadze (1837–1907) and Akaki Tsereteli (1840–1915). In the early 20th century the Georgian symbolist poets experimented with new forms of poetic expression. Among these poets were Paolo Iashvili (1894–1937), Titsian Tabidze (1895–1937), and Galaktion Tabidze (1891–1959), whose movement, The Blue Horns (a reaction against realism and civic modes in Georgian literature), thrived during the years of the Georgian independence struggle, from 1918 to 1921. However, Georgian national literature was suppressed during Stalin's reign, and Titsian Tabidze was executed during one of the purges of the 1930s, while Iashvili committed suicide in 1937.

Georgian literature slowly revived after the death of Stalin. Constantine Gamsakhurdia (1891–1975) was the greatest novelist of the immediate post-Stalinist period, and he introduced an unprecedented subtlety to Georgian prose. He explored Georgia's past and culture through historical novels such as *The Hand of the Great Builder* (1942) and *The Flowering of the Vine* (1955).

Otia Ioseliani (b. 1930) is a successful contemporary dramatist whose comedies *Until the Ox Cart Turns Over* and *Six Old Maids and a Man* have been staged in Germany. Chabua Amirejibi (b. 1921) is noted for his narrative power on historical themes, while Otar Chiladze (b. 1933) explores Georgian myth and history through his novels. Lia Sturua (b. 1939) is Georgia's best-known contemporary woman poet.

The Feast of the Three Nobles by Georgian artist Niko Pirosmanishvili.

PAINTING

Painting is a relatively recent art in Georgia, flourishing since the end of the 19th century. Niko Pirosmanishvili (1862–1918), popularly known as Pirosmani, was a self-taught artist who painted in a direct, primitive style. Through his depiction of everyday Georgian life at the turn of the 20th century, he expressed the national psyche better than any other Georgian artist. He died in obscurity and his work was recognized only after his death. His paintings, such as *Woman and Children Going to Draw Water*, can be viewed at the Georgian State Art Museum in Tbilisi.

Georgian painting flourished throughout the 20th century. Mose Toidze (b. 1902) painted in the Socialist Realist style promoted by the Soviet authorities. Lado Gudiashvili (1896–1980) and David Kakabadze (1889–1952) both painted in a distinctly Georgian style, which is based on Byzantine traditions. Gudiashvili is famous for his fantastic and grotesque portrayals, especially *Fish* (1920) and *The Underprivileged* (1930). Kakabadze created skillful abstract works. Helena Ahklevediani (1901–76) is known for her depictions of historic Tbilisi.

The Georgian zest for living is reflected in their colorful costumes and vibrant dances.

MUSIC AND BALLET

Tbilisi has long had musical connections. Zakaria Paliashvili (1872–1933) is considered the father of Georgian opera. His most famous works are *Abesalom and Eteri* and *Daisi*. Tbilisi's marvelous Moorish opera house, the Paliashvili Opera and Ballet Theater, was named in his honor. His contemporary Meliton Balanchivadze (1862–1937) is also considered one of the originators of Georgian professional music. He wrote the country's first national opera, *Perfidious Daredzhan*, first staged in Tbilisi in 1926. His son, Andrei Balanchivadze (b. 1906), continued the family's musical tradition by writing the first Georgian ballet, *Heart of the Hills*, in 1936, and a composition called *The Pages of Life* in 1961.

Dmitri Arakishvili (1873–1953) brought Georgian folk music into the mainstream, writing and composing more than 500 pieces. He also composed a number of symphonies and choral works.

Vakhtang Chabukiani (b. 1910) is Georgia's most famous ballet dancer and choreographer. After a distinguished dancing career, he became director of the ballet troupe at the Paliashvili Opera and Ballet Theater, where he created a unique style of male stage dancing that combined the movements of both classical ballet and Georgian folk dancing.

Nina Ananiashvili (b. 1963) is artistic director of the State Ballet of Georgia (SBG). Under her leadership, the SBG is enjoying an artistic resurgence. A native of Tbilisi, Ananiashvili has won most of the major awards in ballet and has performed with almost every prestigious ballet company in the world. She has been named a People's Artist of the Georgian Republic.

Tengis Abuladze, director of the movie *Repentance*, with the lead actress, Ketevan Abuladze.

FILM

Under the Soviet regime a strong Georgian movie industry developed and prospered. A former sculptor named Mikhail Chiaureli helped the Georgian branch of Soviet cinema develop during the 1920s and 1930s.

In the post-Stalin era cinema is the only artistic field where Georgian genius has reached its former heights. Like many other forms of artistic expression in Georgia, cinema became a way for people to celebrate their national spirit and culture. Many talented directors have worked in the Gruzia movie studios in Tbilisi. Giorgi Shengelaya (b. 1937) directed *Pirosmani* (1971), a movie that celebrates the life of the famous painter Niko Pirosmanichvili; *Eliso*, based on a short story by Alexander Kazbegi; and *The Blue Mountains*, a satire about the Soviet bureaucracy.

The most famous movie to come out of Georgia in the *perestroika* (restructuring) period (1980–91) was *Repentance* (1984; *Monanieba* in Georgian), an allegory that achieved notoriety for its grotesque depiction of the repressive era under Stalin. Directed by Tengis Abuladze, the movie attracted record audiences all over the Soviet Union, with 17 million people seeing it within the first three weeks of its release. Abuladze had previously won a prize at the Cannes Film Festival in 1956 for the movie *Magdana's Donkey*, a collaboration with his childhood friend Revez Chkeidze (b. 1926). He also won the Lenin Prize for his trilogy *The Plea*, *The Wishing Tree*, and *Repentance*.

LEISURE

ABOVE ALL ELSE, Georgians like to enjoy life. There is a well-known Georgian legend that says much about Georgian attitudes, lifestyle, and leisure. The tale tells of how the Georgians came to possess the country they deem the most beautiful in the world. When the world was being created, God was allotting land to the peoples of the world. The Georgians, who were too busy eating, drinking, and having a good time, showed up late. "There's no land left," God told them.

"But we were drinking a toast to your health," answered the Georgians, "Come and join us."

It is said that God enjoyed himself so much that he gave the Georgians all the land he had been saving for himself. This tale suggests much about the Georgians' high regard for their homeland.

Above: **Georgia's beautiful mountains, lakes, and beaches are enjoyed as much by the local Georgians as they are by the visiting tourists.**

Opposite: **Some youths enjoying a playground ride in Tbilisi.**

When the Georgians are not eating, drinking, and entertaining, they enjoy the kind of leisure activities that are common throughout the world. Radio and television are popular, and people often visit some of Georgia's many museums, especially in Tbilisi, that display the country's rich cultural and artistic heritage. In summer there are many parks and nature reserves where people can walk, climb, or picnic. The most famous of these are at Pitsunda, Borzhomi, and the Forest Park of the Sukhumi Mountains.

SONG AND DANCE

Many Georgian national characteristics emerge in the people's dancing, which is elegant, lively, and flamboyant. Traditional dance is still a part of everyday life in the republic, and Georgians of all ages need very little excuse to begin dancing—they dance on any and every occasion.

Traditional dancers twirling around in their brightly colored outfits.

Traditional Georgian dance is chiefly masculine in form, although a few dances are exclusively for women.

The male dances are energetic, involving much high-kicking, leaping, twisting, and acrobatics. The Fundruki (FOON-dru-ki) is a traditional dance performed by men on the tips of their toes. The Khorumi (Ko-ru-mi) is performed by a circle of men. The dance movements portray combat scenes; the men rear up like horses or creep as though they are hiding behind rocks. The women's dances are less energetic, reflecting a more passive role. The women move their bodies slowly and gracefully. The Lekouri (le-KO-u-ri) is a courtship dance performed by men and women. The dancers do not touch, but circle cautiously, flirting with each other.

Almost every village and valley has its own traditional songs and dances. Often the dances are based on a dramatic local or national occurrence from Georgia's long and eventful history. Folk song and folk dance have developed together in Georgia.

The Rustavi Choir specializes in restoring the folk music traditions of Georgia, scouring the country for half-forgotten songs that its members decipher and record before setting to music.

The republic has many professional song and dance ensembles, including the Georgian State Dancing Company, which has showcased Georgian dances to more than 50 million people in 87 countries.

MOUNTAIN SPORTS AND PASTIMES

Skiing is a popular pastime in Georgia. Situated in Kartli in the Lesser Caucasus, Bakuriani is one of the chief ski resorts and was, during the Soviet era, one of the most popular and famous downhill skiing complexes in the Soviet Union. The resort is 6,000 feet (1,830 m) above sea level and has been likened to Squaw Valley (California) in the United States for its ideal climate and conditions. Another major ski resort is at Gudauri, north of Tbilisi on the Georgian Military Highway. Built and operated as a joint Georgian-Austrian venture, Gudauri is a sparkling new complex of hotels, sports facilities, and superb downhill runs.

Climbing is also a popular sport. It attracts both locals and international climbers. Because of its high peaks, Upper Svaneti is a popular place to climb, and it has produced some of the most famous mountaineers in Georgia. One of the best-known was Mikheil Khergiani (1932–69), who died in a climbing accident. His house in Mestia has been turned into a museum that honors his achievements. His father, Beknu Khergiani, has the distinction of being the climber who removed the Nazi flag from the top of Mount Elbrus after it had been planted there by the advancing Germans in 1943.

Nartaa members taking part in a friendly bout of arm wrestling.

A group of childen playing street soccer.

Another popular spot for alpinists and explorers are the slopes of Mount Kazbek, especially because of the great number of legends and myths associated with the mountain. One legend says that the Georgian Prometheus, Amirani, was chained in a cave on the mountainside as punishment for giving fire to humankind.

OTHER SPORTS

As in many parts of the world, soccer is Georgia's most popular sport. Home games are played in the capital's 78,000-capacity Boris Paichadze National Stadium, also known as the Dinamo Stadium, a soccer stadium in Tbilisi, Georgia. During the 1970s and 1980s the Dinamo Tbilisi team won championships in the Soviet league and also played in European competitions. Kutaisi, Batumi, and Sukhumi also have well-supported soccer teams. Georgia produces many top-class soccer players, many of whom have moved abroad to play in the major European leagues

CHESS

Throughout the former Soviet Union, chess is a very popular pastime, and Georgia is no exception. The Georgians have been very successful in international competitions, and the women, in particular, have excelled in international chess. Nona Gaprindashvili was the women's world chess champion for 16 years, from 1962 to 1978. Another Georgian, Maya Chiburdanidze, who became the women's world champion at the age of 17, eventually ousted Gaprindashvili from her long reign. Chiburdanidze was women's world champion for 13 years, from 1978 to 1991. Gaprindashvili and Chiburdanidze have the distinction of being the only two women to hold the title of Grandmaster in both women's and men's chess.

Among the men, Tamaz Georgadze has performed well in international and Russian chess competitions, and won the international title of Grandmaster in 1977. Since the breakup of the Soviet Union, Georgia has fielded its own chess teams at international competitions.

centered in Germany and England. Georgia has its own rugby federation, and that sport is becoming increasingly popular.

Georgia boasts its own unique form of wrestling. Part sport and part dance, the wrestling is unusual because it is performed to music. It resembles judo in that the contestants are not permitted to use chokeholds or fight while they are lying down. Georgians have also gained wrestling honors on the world stage. As a part of the Soviet team, Levan Tediashvili was both the Olympic and world champion in the 1970s. Georgi Kharebava was the world champion in 1997. The Republic of Georgia won the team titles in men's freestyle and Greco-Roman wrestling in the 2003 World Championships.

A number of traditional folk games are still played in Georgia. *Tskhenburti* (ts-KEN-bur-ti), or "horse ball," is played on horseback by both men and women. It is similar to polo, which is also popular in the nation.

In addition to Georgia's own Black Sea health resorts, Sochi, located in neighboring Russia, also along the Black Sea coast, is a popular summer destination.

HEALTH RESORTS

Georgia's Black Sea coast is the location of many resort towns and beaches, and this is where many Georgians like to spend time relaxing, especially in summer. During the Soviet era government departments from all over Russia had holiday homes reserved for the use of their staff, and every summer people from all parts of the Soviet Union descended upon Georgia's beaches.

Known as Bichvinta in Georgian and Pitsunda in Russian, the republic's most famous Black Sea resort was named after the unique pine grove that is indigenous to the area. The pine grove borders a 4-mile (6.4-km) stretch of beach that is packed each summer. The sunny Abkhazian climate, the beach, the pleasant smell of pine needles, and a 10th-century church make Pitsunda one of the most popular resort towns. Because of the conflict in Abkhazia, it is less accessible than it used to be, although the cessation of hostilities should ensure its continued popularity.

BATH TIME

Tbilisi is famous for its hot sulfur baths. Rich in hydrogen sulfide, the waters have curative effects that have been appreciated by both locals and travelers through the centuries. The baths have been associated with Tbilisi throughout its history, and are said to be the reason why King Vakhtang Gorgasali moved his capital here. In the 12th century as many as 68 different baths drew upon the plentiful underground waters.

There are many sulfur baths in Tbilisi, but the best known is the Herekle bath, situated underground and covered with a grand, domed roof. Many Georgians go to the baths to relax and subject themselves to a rigorous body massage. This massage includes being laid on a stone slab, having their bodies slapped and pummeled, being rubbed with a horsehair mitten (to remove dead skin cells), getting soaped, and finally being rinsed with a bucket of warm water.

French author Alexandre Dumas (1802–70), in *Adventures in Caucasia*, described the experience: "Suddenly, when I least expected it, two attendants seized me, laid me out on a wooden bench and began to crack every single joint in my body, one after the other. Although I felt no discomfort, I was convinced they were all dislocated, and half expected that at any moment, these silent Persians would fold me up like a towel and pop me away in a cupboard. Then one of them held me still while the other positively danced up and down my whole body. He must have weighed a hundred and twenty pounds or more, but he seemed as light as a butterfly. A great sense of freedom and well-being permeated me. All my tiredness had gone and I felt strong enough to lift a mountain."

BORZHOMI MOUNTAIN RETREAT Borzhomi is immediately identified with the curative spring water of the same name, well known both inside and outside of Georgia. Situated in the beautiful Borzhomi Gorge in southwest Kartli on the River Kura, the town of Borzhomi is the largest and best-known mountain spa in the country. The town is home to numerous sanatoriums to which many Georgians go in the summer for a three-week "cure." The fresh mountain air, mineral waters, pleasant climate, and rich forests provide the ideal atmosphere for rest and recreation. Georgians swear by the healing effects of the water, which is also a popular drink.

The Russians built the town in the 19th century, and they quickly discovered it to be the perfect retreat from the stresses of running an empire. Russian influence is reflected in the 19th-century carved wooden houses of the area.

"Never in my life have I encountered either in Russia or in Turkey anything more luxurious than the Tiflis baths."

—Alexander Pushkin (1799–1837), Russian poet, on the Tbilisi baths. Tiflis is the old name for Tbilisi, transliterated from Russian.

FESTIVALS

DURING THE SOVIET ERA Georgia celebrated many festivals such as Labor Day, Soviet National Day, and World War II Victory Day along with the rest of the Soviet Union. Since independence, however, traditional Georgian festivals have been revived. The old, Soviet-inspired festivals are now celebrated on a much smaller scale or have been dispensed with altogether. The patriotic Georgians prefer to celebrate their own folk festivals and those linked to the Georgian Orthodox Church.

Although the Soviet Union was officially atheist and religious festivals were frowned on, the popularity of the Georgian Orthodox Church never truly declined. The Georgian Church became, to some extent, a focus for Georgian nationalism during the Soviet era. It is no surprise, then, that with the demise of the Soviet Union and Georgia's ensuing independence, Orthodox festivals have sharply increased in popularity and are celebrated with great enthusiasm.

Left: **A musician playing at the Kolhoba festival celebration in a village within Adjaria.**

Opposite: **Candle offerings and prayers made during Saint Miriam's Day.**

A woman decorating an Easter egg.

GEORGIAN ORTHODOX AND FOLK HOLIDAYS

Some folk and religious holidays are celebrated nationally, while others are peculiar to a town or region. In keeping with the spirit of people who enjoy feasting, a meal and festivities in the town or neighborhood square follow almost all religious services and festivals, and drinking and toasting continue late into the night.

The Georgian Orthodox Church celebrates all the major feast days of the Orthodox calendar. The Georgian Church, like the Russian Orthodox Church, follows the Julian calendar, which is 13 days behind the Gregorian calendar used by most of the world.

The Feast of Saint Basil the Great is celebrated on January 1 throughout Georgia. Saint Basil (329–79) was one of the great spiritual fathers of the Eastern Orthodox Church, and because of this, he is feted throughout the Orthodox world. As in other Orthodox countries, Christmas is celebrated on January 6 in Georgia, according to the church calendar.

Easter is by far the most important festival on the Georgian Orthodox calendar, as it is for all Orthodox churches. Women and children prepare and dye Easter eggs, which are a symbol of renewal and rebirth. As with all Georgian festivals, family and friends gather after the church service to celebrate with a feast. Ascension Day—commemorating the ascension of Christ into heaven—is observed 40 days after Easter. Candles are extinguished as part of the church ritual to symbolize Christ's physical departure from this world.

Saint Nino, who introduced Christianity to Georgia, is honored in May. Church services and feasts also mark the birth of Saint John the Baptist on June 24, and the remembrance of Saints Peter and Paul on June 28. The Assumption—Saint Miriam's Day (another name for the Virgin Mary)—is celebrated on August 28 in memory of the death of the Virgin Mary and the belief that she was taken up bodily into heaven.

Mtskheta's Day is observed on October 14. Mtskheta is Georgia's oldest city and the center of ancient Iberian culture. The Georgians believe that the city was named after Mtskhetos, son of Kartlos, the mythical father of the Georgian people. On Mtskheta's Day the congregation throngs in the Cathedral of Sveti-tskhoveli. This is one of the most sacred places in Georgia and is the center of the Georgian Orthodox Church. The patriarch leads a procession around the cathedral grounds, carrying banners and icons. Bells are rung to celebrate the occasion. In the town, clowns, mimes, and wrestlers entertain the people.

Saint George, the patron saint of Georgia, is honored on November 23. This is a very popular feast day because Saint George is not only a Christian symbol but also a national figure who represents the country's warlike pre-Christian past.

Many folk festivals are celebrated locally at various times of the year. On the third Sunday after Easter, for example, a special holiday in honor of Saint George is celebrated in Tbilisi and many parts of Kartli, Kakheti, Imereti, and Svaneti. Another festival is Okanoba (o-ka-NO-ba), held to mark the day Iberia adopted the Christian faith. This occurs in Gori and other parts of Kartli on the day after Easter.

A Christian painting at the Lavia Monastery. Christian Georgians celebrate numerous Orthodox holidays and festivals.

In the major wine-producing regions of Kakheti and Imereti, it is traditional to hold festivals and celebrate the harvest while gathering the grapes in October. Balconies and windows are decorated with bunches of grapes, and songs and dancing take place when the day's work is done.

OTHER RELIGIOUS FESTIVALS

Georgia's Muslim population celebrates all the major Islamic festivals, such as Eid-al-Fitr—a celebration to mark the end of the fasting month of Ramadan—and Eid-al-Adha, the Prophet Muhammad's birthday. Georgia's small Jewish community celebrates all the major Jewish festivals.

CIVIL HOLIDAYS

Georgians still celebrate a number of civil holidays that have survived from the Soviet era. May 1 is celebrated as Labor Day throughout the Commonwealth of Independent States, and in Georgia it is a popular spring holiday.

Georgians also observe World War II Victory Day on May 9 by laying wreaths and paying their respects to those who lost their lives in the war. During Soviet rule it was a common practice to have holidays to celebrate the achievements of certain public services, such as industry or the military. Some of these days are still observed, such as Georgian Police Day (November 22), which includes a parade of police vehicles through Tbilisi. Mother's Day has replaced the more politicized Soviet celebration of International Women's Day in March.

TBILISOBA

The Festival of Tbilisi, Tbilisoba (t-BLI-so-ba), occurs on the last Sunday in October to commemorate the founding of Tbilisi and all things Georgian. The festival, which is the largest annual celebration in Tbilisi, is marked with a street carnival, and many of Georgia's famous song-and-dance ensembles put on traditional Georgian performances. The celebration is not complete without the traditional personification of old Tbilisi—the roguish Kinto—clowning with a wine skin.

The festival was suspended for a few years as a sign of protest and national mourning following the tragic killing of 20 demonstrators in Tbilisi by Soviet Special Forces on April 9, 1989.

INDEPENDENCE DAY Georgians celebrate their independence on May 26. This day marks the country's first independence in 1918 following the 1917 Russian Revolution and the subsequent disintegration of tsarist Russia. Traditionally and historically this date is more significant to the Georgians than their break with the Soviet Union in 1991.

In recent years Independence Day has been marked by noisy displays of military strength with troops, artillery, and tanks parading down Rustaveli Avenue in Tbilisi, while warplanes fly overhead. In the early 1990s various paramilitary groups, such as the Mkhedrioni (m-ked-RIO-ni), participated in the official procession. More recently the Mkhedrioni's absence is a positive sign of the waning power of warlords and the growing strength and stability of the elected government.

Street parade during a Tbilisoba festival.

FOOD

ALTHOUGH GEORGIAN COOKING has a distinct flavor, the ingredients and style bear some similarity to the cuisines of the eastern Mediterranean. Georgian food may be little known in the West, but it is one of the most varied and subtle cuisines of the former Soviet Union.

The country's sunny climate and fertile soil have traditionally resulted in an abundance of homegrown agricultural produce. Most food is bought fresh from the market. Georgians are not used to eating frozen or processed food. Although multinational fast-food outlets selling hamburgers and fried chicken exist in Georgia, they have yet to achieve the kind of popularity they have in the West or in other countries in the Commonwealth of Independent States, such as Russia. Classic Georgian meal ingredients include lamb, chicken, fish, hazelnuts, walnuts, corn, pomegranates, plums, grapes, kidney beans, peppers, coriander, and mint. There are many regional variations.

Above: **Fruit store vendors with their fresh produce.**

Opposite: **A poultry vendor at the Central Market.**

THE GEORGIAN TABLE

Although there are many good restaurants in Georgia's towns and cities, the best place to experience the full range of Georgian cuisine is in the home. Georgians love entertaining, and they invite relatives, colleagues, friends, and even strangers into their homes at the slightest opportunity. Entertaining at the table offers Georgians the chance to express their generosity, exuberance, and sense of community. For Georgians a good meal is a well-attended table groaning under the weight of vast amounts of food and drink.

Shashlyk **is traditionally prepared by men.**

At home women cook and serve the food. The men do not help. Instead they sit at the head of the table toasting and entertaining guests. Georgian food is not served in conventional courses or even in any particular order. Soup may make its appearance an hour into the meal, and great platefuls of *shashlyk* (shash-LIK), or skewers of grilled lamb, and roast pork may appear late in a meal.

MEAT Georgia is a predominantly mountainous country where people mostly raise sheep and chicken, and this is reflected in the cuisine. *Shashlyk*, better known elsewhere as "shish kebab," is the most popular meat dish in the Caucasus, although chicken is also popular. *Chakhobili* (cha-ko-BI-li) is a chicken and tomato stew spiced with coriander, while *tabaka* (TA-ba-ka) is cooked by frying chicken that has been pressed between two clay plates. *Khinkali* (KIN-ka-li), or dumplings filled with ground lamb, chicken, or beef, is a local favorite. *Basturma* (BAS-tur-ma) is a thinly sliced and seasoned air-dried beef.

VEGETABLE DISHES Although the Georgian diet is heavily meat-based, vegetables accompany most meals. *Pkhala* (p-KA-la) is a spiced spinach dish mixed with walnuts and vinegar, and topped with pomegranate seeds. It is generally eaten with *matsoni* (MA-tso-ni), or Georgian yogurt, and *lavashi* (LA-va-shi), a flat, flaky bread.

Lobio (LO-bi-o) consists of kidney beans baked with water and then crushed with a pestle and mixed with coriander and spices. This is often eaten as an accompaniment to meat dishes. Eggplant is also a popular ingredient. *Badrijani* (bad-RI-ja-ni) consists of baby eggplants stuffed with ground hazelnuts and herbs, served whole. *Chanakhi* (CHA-na-ki) is a mixture of eggplants, tomatoes, green peppers, and chunks of lamb cooked in a clay pot. Vine leaves stuffed with rice, herbs, and minced lamb are a popular dish throughout the Caucasus and are served with yogurt.

A serving of popular Adjarian meat and vegetable dishes.

***Suluguni*, a cheese made from goat's milk.**

CHEESE AND BREAD Georgian cheese is generally made from goat's milk. There are many varieties, but *suluguni* (su-LU-gu-ni) is a typical Georgian cheese that resembles mozzarella. *Khachapuri* (kach-A-pu-ri) is a cheese pastry made by wrapping *suluguni* cheese in pieces of dough and baking them. This local equivalent of fast food is sold by street vendors and in cafés and restaurants. Bread is served as an accompaniment to all meals. Called *puri* (PU-ri), it is either round and crusty or long and doughlike. The latter variety is known as *dedaspuri* (de-das-PU-ri). *Lavashi* (the flat, flaky bread) is often eaten with yogurt.

SAUCES Sauces are used extensively at the Georgian table to complement, rather than mask, the primary ingredient. *Satsivi* (SA-tsi-vi), better known as the Turkish Circassian sauce, is made of ground walnuts and is generally used to accompany poached chicken. *Adzhika* (AD-zi-ka) is a hot condiment from Abkhazia made from red chilies and herbs, while *tkhemali* (t-KE-ma-li) is a spicy plum sauce that is considered an essential accompaniment for *shashlyk*. Pomegranate chutney is also used to accompany lamb and fish dishes.

A selection of soft drinks available in Georgia.

DRINKS

Georgia's varied climate means that the humid regions of Samegrelo and Adjaria are able to grow subtropical plants such as tea, while the drier central and eastern parts of the country can grow grapes for winemaking. Georgian tea is of the green variety, and is drunk at home and in teahouses. Thick, strong, Turkish coffee is also popular. Because of Turkey's historical influence in Adjaria, the best place to drink coffee is in one of Batumi's many cafés.

Georgia also produces its own brandy and mineral water. Georgian brandies are considered equal in quality to some of the more famous labels from neighboring Armenia. The best-known labels are Vardzia, Sakartvelo, Tbilisi, and Eniseli. Georgia's own mineral water, Borzhomi— from the resort of the same name—is similar to Perrier, although it is saltier and less fizzy. Borzhomi, Georgia's third-largest export, has a daily yield of 110,000 gallons (500,000 l) of mineral water, which is sold throughout the world. *Chacha* (CHA-cha), a home brewed spirit made from grape pulp, is drunk at home.

WINE Georgia has a long winemaking tradition. Archaeological evidence suggests that wine was made as far back as 5000 B.C., making Georgia one of the ancient centers of viticulture. The most famous wine-growing regions are Kakheti, Imereti, Racha, and Lechkhumi. Abkhazia also produces some good wines. Although most of the wine is produced on

A man in Kakheti prepares jars for the new season's wine.

farms, many residents of these regions have their own garden grapevines, as well as huge tubs for treading the grapes and vats for fermenting the wine. The grapes are harvested in early October.

Georgia grows more than 500 grape varieties—a vast array for such a small country—and produces 60 different wines. Protected by the Caucasus, the republic's numerous valleys—each with its own microclimate—have ideal conditions for growing many types of grapes. The best grape varieties are Saperavi, Tsinandali, Chinuri, Mtsvane, and Tasitska. Most Georgian wines are named after the region or town in which they are produced.

The most popular white wines are Gurdzhaani and Tsinandali; the latter is the pride of Georgian wines, and is grown in the Alazani Valley in Kakheti, a region famous for its good wines. The most popular red wines are Mukuzani and Napareuli (both made from the Saperavi grape), Ojaleshi, and Khvanchkara. The last of these has the dubious distinction of being Stalin's favorite. Rkatsiteli is a dry white wine produced in Kardanakhi in Kakheti. Among Georgian wines, it claims the peculiar distinction of being fermented in clay jars buried underground—a unique Kakhetian practice.

During the Soviet era Georgia produced a large part of the domestic wine consumed in the Soviet Union. During the last decade Georgian wine producers have attempted to break into world markets, tailoring their wines to international standards.

GEORGIAN *SUPRAS*

Supra, a traditional Georgian feast, is an important part of Georgian social culture. There are two types of *supra*: a festivity *supra* called Keipi and a somber *supra* called Kelekhi, which is always held after burials.

CHAKHOBILI (GEORGIAN MEAT AND TOMATO STEW)

2 pounds (1 kg) chicken or lamb, cubed
1 tablespoon vegetable or olive oil
2 onions, chopped
2 cans, 1 pound (400 g) each, whole tomatoes
3 large potatoes, peeled and cubed
1 teaspoon salt
1 teaspoon ground pepper
2 teaspoons coriander, ground
1–2 teaspoons dried parsley
1 teaspoon dried basil leaves
5 cloves crushed garlic

Heat oil in a casserole. Add meat and cook for 10 minutes, or until browned. Add chopped onions and stir until soft. Add tomatoes, and crush them with the back of a wooden spoon. Stir in cubed potatoes, salt, and pepper. Cover the casserole and simmer over a low heat for about 45 minutes, or until meat and potatoes are tender, and tomatoes have formed a sauce-like consistency. If the mixture starts to dry out too much as it cooks, add some boiled water. Uncover and turn up heat and stir in the herbs and crushed garlic. Continue to stir as the sauce bubbles for 10 minutes. Remove the casserole from heat, cover, and leave to stand for 5–8 minutes before serving.

GOZINAKE (CANDIED WALNUTS)

(Makes about two dozen pieces of candy)

3½ cups of walnuts, shelled and ground
1 cup of honey

Toast walnuts lightly at 350°F (175°C) for 10 minutes, then chop them coarsely. In a deep saucepan bring honey to a boil. Stir in nuts and cook over medium heat for 8–10 minutes, stirring occasionally, until mixture is thick. Be careful not to let it burn. Pour the mixture out onto a moistened wooden board or oiled marble slab. With a spatula, spread it ½-inch (1.27-cm) thick. When cool, cut into 2-inch (5-cm) diamonds.

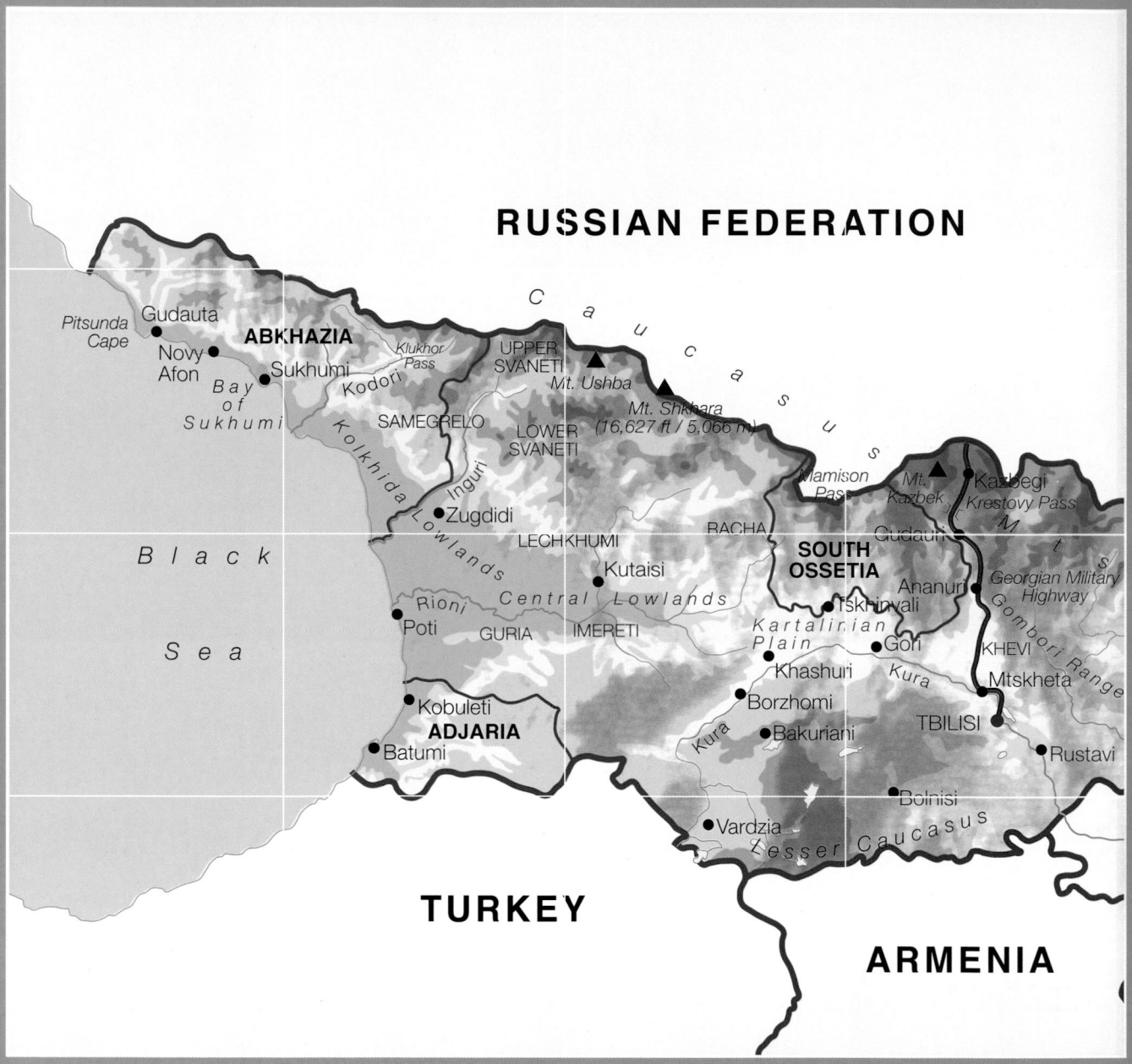
A
B
C
D
1
2
3
4
RUSSIAN FEDERATION
Caucasus
Pitsunda Cape
Gudauta
ABKHAZIA
Novy Afon
Sukhumi
Bay of Sukhumi
Klukhor Pass
Kodori
UPPER SVANETI
Mt. Ushba
Mt. Shkhara (16,627 ft / 5,066 m)
SAMEGRELO
LOWER SVANETI
Kolkhida Lowlands
Inguri
Zugdidi
Mamison Pass
Mt. Kazbek
Kazbegi
Krestovy Pass
Gudauri
RACHA
SOUTH OSSETIA
LECHKHUMI
Kutaisi
Black Sea
Rioni
Poti
GURIA
Central Lowlands
IMERETI
Tskhinvali
Ananuri
Georgian Military Highway
Kartalinian Plain
Gori
KHEVI
Gombori Range
Khashuri
Kura
Mtskheta
Kobuleti
ADJARIA
Borzhomi
Bakuriani
TBILISI
Batumi
Rustavi
Bolnisi
Vardzia
Lesser Caucasus
TURKEY
ARMENIA

MAP OF GEORGIA

Abkhazia, A1–A2, B1–B2
Adjaria, A3, B2–B3
Alazani River, C2, D2–D3
Ananuri, C2
Armenia, B3, C3, D3
Azerbaijan, C3, D2–D3

Bakuriani, B3
Batumi, A3
Bay of Sukhumi, A2
Black Sea, A1–A3, B2–B3
Bolnisi, C3
Borzhomi, B2, C2

Caucasus Mts., B1–B2, C2
Central lowlands, B2

Georgian Military Highway, C2
Gombori Range, C2–C3
Gori, C2
Gudauri, C2
Gudauta, A1
Gurdzaani, D3
Guria, B2

Imereti, B2
Inguri River, B2
Iori Plateau, D3
Iori River, C2–C3, D3

Kartalinian Plain, B2, C2
Kazbegi, C2
Kazbek, Mt., C2
Khashuri, B2, C2
Khevi, C2
Klukhor Pass, B1
Kobuleti, B2
Kodori River, A2, B2
Kolkhida Lowlands, A2, B2
Krestvovy Pass, C2
Kura River, B2-B3, C2
Kutaisi, B2

Lechkhumi, B2
Lesser Caucasus, B3, C3
Lower Svaneti, B2

Mamison Pass, C2
Mtskheta, C2
Novy Afon, A1

Pitsunda Cape, A1
Poti, B2

Racha, B2
Rioni River, B2
Russian Federation, A1, B1–B2, C1–C2, D1–D3
Rustavi, C3

Samegrelo, A2, B2
South Ossetia, C2
Shkhara, Mt., B2
Sukhumi, A2

Tbilisi, C3
Telavi, D2
Tskhinvali, C2
Turkey, A3, B3, C3

Upper Svaneti, B1–B2
Ushba, Mt., B1–B2

Vardzia, B3

Zugdidi, B2

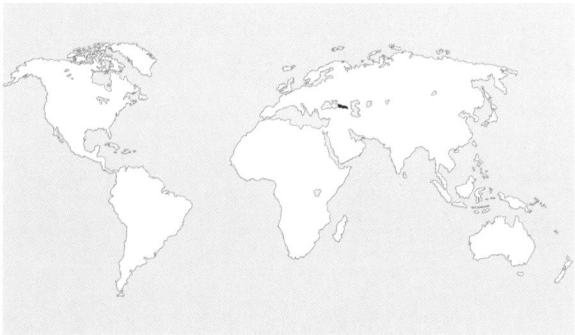

ECONOMIC GEORGIA

Manufacturing

- Coal
- Timber
- Wine

Agriculture

- Cattle farming
- Citrus fruits
- Corn
- Grapes
- Hazelnuts
- Potatoes
- Tea
- Tobacco
- Vegetables

Natural Resources

- Gas
- Hydropower
- Metals
- Minerals
- Oil

Services

- Airport
- Seaports
- Tourism
- Train stations

ABOUT THE ECONOMY

Georgia's main activities include the cultivation of grapes, citrus fruits, and hazelnuts for export. Concerted reform efforts have helped the economy achieve positive GDP growth and reduce inflation. The construction of the BTC oil pipeline and the BTE gas pipeline has brought much-needed investment and job opportunities. Georgia pins its hope for long-term growth on its role as a transit state for pipelines and trade. Tourism is another source of revenue for modern Georgia, given its climate and topography. A major challenge is finding alternative energy supplies and improving the infrastructure of its energy sector.

GROSS DOMESTIC PRODUCT (GDP)
$9.553 billion (2007 estimate)

GDP GROWTH
12 percent (2007 estimate)

INFLATION RATE
11 percent (2007 estimate)

CURRENCY
Lari (GEL)
1 U.S. dollar = 1.77 lari (2008)
1 Lari (GEL) = 100 Tetri
Notes: 1, 2, 5, 10, 20, 50, and 100 lari
Coins: 1, 2, 5, 10, 20, and 50 tetri
Notes are in denominations of 1, 2, 5, 10, 20, 50, and 100 lari.
Coins are in denominations of 1, 2, 5, 10, 20, and 50 tetri.

NATURAL RESOURCES
Forests, hydropower, nonferrous metals, manganese, iron ore, copper

AGRICULTURAL PRODUCTS
Citrus fruits, grapes, tea, hazelnuts, vegetables, livestock

INDUSTRY
Steel, aircraft, machine tools, electrical appliances, mining (manganese and copper), chemicals, wood products, wine

MAJOR EXPORTS
Scrap metal, machinery, chemicals, fuel reexports, citrus fruits, tea, wine

MAJOR IMPORTS
Fuels, machinery and parts, transportation equipment, grain and other foods, pharmaceuticals

EXPORT PARTNERS
Turkey, Azerbaijan, Russia, Armenia, Turkmenistan, Bulgaria, United States, Ukraine, Canada, Germany (2006)

IMPORT PARTNERS
Russia, Turkey, Germany, Ukraine, Azerbaijan (2006)

POPULATION BELOW POVERTY LINE
31 percent (2006 estimate)

WORKFORCE
2.02 million (2007 estimate)

UNEMPLOYMENT RATE
13.6 percent (2006)

CULTURAL GEORGIA

ABOUT THE CULTURE

OFFICIAL NAME
Georgia (Sak'art'velo in Georgian)

FLAG DESCRIPTION
A single right-angled red cross connects all the sides of a rectangular white flag. In each of the four white corners are four smaller red bolnur-katskhuri crosses. The five-cross flag appears to date back to the 14th century. The crosses symbolize Jesus Christ and the four evangelists. The white background is a sign of innocence, chastity, purity, and wisdom. The red color of the cross stands for courage, bravery, justice, and love.

CAPITAL
Tbilisi

POPULATION
4.6 million (2007 estimate)

BIRTHRATE
10.5 births per 1,000 Georgians (2007 estimate)

DEATH RATE
9.4 deaths per 1,000 Georgians (2007 estimate)

AGE DISTRIBUTION
Under 15: 16.7 percent; 15–64: 66.6 percent; 65 and over: 16.7 percent (2007 estimates)

ETHNIC GROUPS
Georgian 83.8 percent, Azerbaijani 6.5 percent, Armenian 5.7 percent, Russian 1.5 percent, Ossetian 0.9 percent, Other 1.6 percent (2002 estimates)

RELIGIOUS GROUPS
Georgian Orthodox 83.9 percent, Armenian Apostolic 3.9 percent, Catholic 0.8 percent, Muslim 9.9 percent, Other (mostly nonreligious) 1.5 percent (2002 estimates)

MAIN LANGUAGES
Georgian (official), Russian, Armenian, Azeri, Abkhaz (official language in Abkhazia)

LITERACY RATE
Virtually 100 percent (2004 estimate)

IMPORTANT HOLIDAYS

January 1	The Feast of Saint Basil the Great; New Year
January 6	Orthodox Christmas
March–April	Good Friday–Easter Sunday
May 26	Independence Day
August 28	The Virgin's Assumption (Saint Miriam's Day)
October 14	Mtskheta's Day
October (last Sunday)	Tbilisoba
November 23	Saint George's Day

TIME LINE

IN GEORGIA	IN THE WORLD
A.D. 683 to 685 Khazar soldiers invades Transcaucasia, inflicting much damage, and stealing much booty.	
	A.D. 1000 The Chinese perfect gunpowder and begin to use it in warfare.
1089 to 1125 King David the Builder's reign increases Georgia's wealth and prestige.	
	1100 Rise of the Incan civilization in Peru
1172 to 1216 Medieval poet Shota Rustaveli writes *Vepkhistkaosani*, the Georgian national epic poem.	
1178 King Giorgi III crowns his teenage daughter Tamar as co-ruler.	
1204 to 1205 Queen Tamar and her soldiers overcome the Turks at the Battle of Basiani.	**1206–1368** Genghis Khan unifies the Mongols and starts conquest of the world. At its height, the Mongol Empire under Kublai Khan stretches from China to Persia and parts of Europe and Russia.
1212 Queen Tamar dies after a 24-year reign.	
1236 Queen Rusudani, daughter of Queen Tamar, flees as Mongol hordes ravishes Georgia.	**1558–1603** Reign of Elizabeth I of England
1783 Georgia becomes a protectorate of tsarist Russia.	**1789–99** The French Revolution
1801 to 1804 Most of present-day Georgia becomes part of the Russian Empire.	**1869** The Suez Canal is opened.
1918 An independent Georgian state is declared.	**1914** World War I begins.
1921 Soviet troops invade Georgia and Georgia declares itself a Soviet Socialist Republic.	
1936 Armenia, Azerbaijan, Georgia, Kazakh, and Kirghiz become constituent republics of the Soviet Union.	**1939** World War II begins.
1972 Eduard Shevardnadze is appointed head of the Georgian Communist Party.	**1945** The United States drops atomic bombs on Hiroshima and Nagasaki, Japan.
1990 South Ossetia declares itself sovereign.	**1986** Nuclear power disaster at Chernobyl in Ukraine

IN GEORGIA	IN THE WORLD
1991 Georgia declares independence from the Soviet Union. A strong earthquake rocks Georgia and leaves 100,000 people homeless. Zviad Gamsakhurdia is elected president.	**1991** Breakup of the Soviet Union
1993 Georgia becomes a member of Russia's Commonwealth of Independent States.	
1994 Abkhazia declares independence. Vladislav Ardzinba becomes president.	
1995 Eduard Shevardnadze is elected president.	
1999 Pope John Paul II, along with Patriarch Ilia II, visits the Orthodox Church.	**1997** Hong Kong is returned to China.
2000 President Eduard Shevardnadze wins reelection with 82 percent of the vote. Dzhumber Patiashvili, ex-Communist leader, trails with 17 percent and charges that widespread vote rigging had taken place.	
2001 President Shevardnadze fires his government as demonstrators take to the streets and demand changes.	**2001** Terrorists crash planes in New York, Washington D.C., and Pennsylvania.
2003 President Eduard Shevardnadze resigns following the Rose Revolution.	**2003** War in Iraq begins.
2004 Mikhail Saakashvili is inaugurated as president.	
2005 The agreement on the appointment of Partnership for Peace (PfP) liaison officer between Georgia and NATO comes into force.	
2006 The last of Russia's servicemen leaves Tbilisi, ending 200 years of Russian presence.	

GLOSSARY

blate (blatè)
Bending the rules.

brtskinvale (br-ts-kin-VA-le)
Brilliant.

Catholicos
Head of the Georgian Orthodox Church.

chacha (CHA-cha)
Strong, home brewed spirit made from grape pulp.

chakhobili (cha-ko-BI-li)
Chicken and tomato stew.

cherkeska (CHER-kes-kah)
Knee-length tunic.

darbazi (dar-BA-zi)
Rustic houses dating back to ancient times.

Gauma . . . jos! (ga-u-MA . . . jos)
Cheers!

Golden Fleece
The fleece of the golden ram, stolen by Jason and the Argonauts from the king of Colchis.

Kartvelebi (kart-VE-le-bi)
Georgians' name for themselves.

khantsi (KAN-tsi)
Large goat's horn filled with wine.

khinkali (KIN-ka-li)
Bell-shaped dumplings filled with ground lamb, chicken, or beef.

lavashi (LA-va-shi)
Flat, flaky bread.

Mxedruli (m-ked-RU-li)
Georgian script.

Nartaa (NAR-ta)
Famous choir made up of elderly men.

puri (PU-ri)
Bread.

Sakartvelo (sa-KART-ve-lo)
Georgians' name for their country, and a term used for the United Kingdom of Georgia, first formed in A.D. 1008.

satsivi (SA-tsi-vi)
Turkish Circassian sauce.

suluguni (su-LU-gu-ni)
Typical Georgian cheese.

tamada (TA-ma-da)
Toastmaster.

Tiflis
Old name for the capital, Tbilisi, transliterated from Russian.

Transcaucasia
Collective name for the countries of the Caucasus: Georgia, Armenia, and Azerbaijan. Transcaucasia was a republic within the Soviet Union from 1922 to 1936.

trtvili (TR-t-vi-li)
Frost.

FURTHER INFORMATION

BOOKS

Burford, Tim. *Bradt Travel Guide: Georgia*. United Kingdom: Bradt Publications, 2007.

Holubec, Vojtëch and Pavel Kivka. *The Caucasus and Its Flowers*. Prague: Prague Publishing, 2006.

Karumidze, Zurab. *Enough: The Rose Revolution in the Republic of Georgia*. New York: Nova Science Publishers Inc., 2005.

Nasmyth, Peter. *Georgia: In The Mountains of Poetry*. New York: Palgrave Macmillan, 1998.

Piddock, Charles. *Republic of Georgia (Nations in the News)*. Milwaukee, WI: World Almanac Library, 2006.

Rosen, Roger. *Georgia: Sovereign Country of the Caucasus (Odyssey Illustrated Guide)*. Corona, CA: Odyssey Publications, 2004.

Steavenson, Wendell. *Stories I Stole From Georgia*. London: Atlantic Books, 2003.

WEB SITES

About Georgia. http://www.aboutgeorgia.net/geography/; http://www.aboutgeorgia.net/geography/topography.html

Central Eurasian Studies Review. http://www.mapageweb.umontreal.ca/tuitekj/cours/FLORIAN-SUPRA.pdf

Georgian Folk Dance. http://www.youtube.com/watch?v=oe6QbfdA17M&mode=related&search=

Georgian government. www.parliament.ge/pages/archive_en/history/his4.htm

IMDb. www.imdb.com/name/nm0002156

Music from Orthodox Monastery. http://fatherstephen.wordpress.com/2007/08/20/music-from-orthodox-georgia

Nina Ananiashvili. http://georgien.blogspot.com/2007/06/video-nino-nina-ananiashvili-fan-dance.html

Timeline Georgia. http://news.bbc.co.uk/2/hi/europe/country_profiles/1102575.stm

Tourism. http://www.tourism.gov.ge/geo/

UNECE. http://unece.org/env/epr/studies/georgia/welcome.htm; http://unece.org/env/epr/studies/georgia/chapter08.pdf

Music CD

Georgia Kavkasia Trio. *Traditional Songs from Georgia*.

BIBLOGRAPHY

Bitov, Andrei. *A Captive in the Caucasus.* London: Collins Harvill, 1992.

Boyette, Michael and Randi Boyette. *Soviet Georgia.* New York: Chelsea House Publishers, 1989.

Clark, Mary Jane Behrends. *The Commonwealth of Independent States.* Brookfield, CT: Millbrook Press, 1992.

Iskander, Fasel. *Gospel According to Chegem.* New York: Vintage Books, 1984.

Nasmyth, Peter. *Georgia: A Rebel in the Caucasus.* London: Cassell, 1992.

Roberts, Elizabeth. *Georgia, Armenia, and Azerbaijan.* Brookfield, CT: Millbrook Press, 1993.

Rosen, Roger. *The Georgian Republic.* Hong Kong: The Guidebook Co. Ltd, 1992.

Russell, Mary. *Please Don't Call It Soviet Georgia.* London: Serpent's Tail, 1991.

Suny, Ronald Grigor. *The Making of the Georgian Nation.* Bloomington, IN: Indiana University Press, 1988.

About Georgia. www.aboutgeorgia.net

Ballet and Nina Ananiashvili. www.opera.ge/eng/administration

Central Intelligence Agency World Factbook (select Georgia Republic from country list). www.cia.gov/library/publications/the-world-factbook/geos/ts.html; https://www.cia.gov/library/publications/the-world-factbook/geos/gg.html

Embassy of Georgia. www.georgiaemb.org/links.asp

Georgia Investment Guide. http://www.investmentguide.ge

Georgian Recipes. www.aboutgeorgia.net/cuisine

Legislation Online. www.legislationline.org

Ministry of Foreign Affairs of Georgia. www.mfa.gov.ge

MSN Encarta-encyclopedia. Uk.encarta.msn.com/text_7615564150/Georgia_(republic).html

One World Journeys. www.oneworldjourneys.com/georgia/enviro_issues.html

The Turkish Press. www.turkishpress.com/news.asp?id=125973

Timeline. www.timelines.ws/countries/georgia

U.S. Department of State. www.state.gov/r/pa/ei/bgn/5253.htm

U.S. Embassy of Georgia. www.georgia.usembassy.gov/events/2006/event20060818

INDEX

Abkhazian Autonomous Republic, 35, 40, 65, 93
Adjaria, 43–44
agriculture, 31, 47, 49, 50
Alazani Valley, 11, 50, 129
architecture, 13, 80, 98, 99, 100, 10
  Baroque Russian, 13
  castle, 99
  darbazi, 98
  fortress, 99
art
  frescoes, 101
  painting, 105

central lowland, 10–11
  Kolkhida lowlands, 10, 16, 63
churches
  Armenian Apostolic Church, 83
  Cathedral of Sveti-tskhoveli, 82
  Georgian Orthodox Church, 79–81
  Russian Orthodox Church, 83
city, 13–14
  Batumi, 14
  Kutaisi, 14
  Rustavi, 14
  Sukhumi, 14
  Tbilisi, 9, 10, 11, 12, 13, 14, 17, 20, 21, 23, 24, 27, 28, 30, 32, 35, 36, 38, 41, 44, 47, 48, 51, 52, 53, 57, 63, 67, 70, 76, 79, 83, 85, 88, 92, 95, 97, 98, 99, 102, 105, 106, 107, 109, 111, 112, 115, 119, 120, 121, 127, 133, 136, 137, 139, 140
climate, 7, 10, 14, 15, 16, 32, 33, 50, 53, 111, 114, 115, 123, 127, 135
  Alpine, 15, 17
  rainfall, 15
  subtropical, 10, 14, 15, 16, 50, 127
  temperature, 15
Commonwealth of Independent States, 33, 45, 66, 120, 123, 139, 142
communications, 9, 28, 48, 58
  mobile telephone, 95
  pager service, 95
  telephone, 95
constitution, 36, 37, 43, 77, 79, 93
  freedom of religious practice, 37
  freedom of speech and thought, 37
  freedom to own property, 37
  human rights, 37
  right to strike, 77

dance, 109, 110, 111, 113, 120, 141
  ballet, 106–107
  traditional, 109–110
    Fundruki, 110
    Khorumi, 110
    Lekouri, 110
deforestation, 55, 56

economic policy, 31
  collectivization, 30, 31
education, 76
elections, 32, 33, 35, 36, 37, 38, 44
endangered species, 17
  dwarf shrew, 17
  goitered gazelle, 17
energy, 47, 52, 58, 135
  hydroelectric, 52
  natural gas, 52
exports, 47, 49

family, 73
fauna, 17
  birds, 17
festivals, 117–121
film, 107
flag, 31, 37, 111, 137
flora, 16–17
forests, 11, 16, 17, 55, 56, 115
  temperate rain forests, 11

gross domestic product, 42, 47, 50, 135

health care, 77
history, 19–33
  Ottoman Turks, 26–27

income, 49
independence, 21, 25, 29, 30, 32, 33, 35, 36, 39, 40, 42, 43, 52 55, 57, 65, 76, 80, 88, 94, 97, 104, 117, 121, 139
  Independence Day, 121
industry, 27, 28, 47, 48, 49, 50, 51, 53, 58, 107, 120
  small cottage industries, 31

languages, 87–95
  dialects, 88
    Acharuli, 88
  Guruli, 88
  Imeruli, 88
  Khaxuri, 88
  Rachuli, 88
  Georgian, 87–89
  Georgian alphabet, 89–90
  Russian, 88
Lesser Caucasus, 8, 11, 25, 100, 111, 133
literature, 102–103
  novelist, 104
  Constantine Gamsakhurdia, 104
  Otar Chiladze, 104
Lower Svaneti, 10, 12, 64, 133

marriage, 73–74
media
  newspapers, 94–95
  periodicals, 94
  radio, 95
  television, 95
metallurgy, 97
military, 32, 33, 36, 39, 42, 45, 101, 120, 121
  Georgian Army, 42
  The National Guard, 42
Mongols, 25, 99, 100, 138
mountains, 7, 9, 11, 13, 15, 16, 17, 52, 55, 100, 109

Bokovoy range, 8
Caucasus mountain range, 7, 8
Great Caucasus range, 8–9
Likhi mountain range, 11, 15
Lomisi, 8
Mount Didi-Abuli, 11
Mount Kazbek, 8, 112
Mount Rustaveli, 9
Mount Shkhara, 8
Mount Tetnuldi, 8
Mount Ushba, 8
museum, 97, 111, 136
Georgian State Museum, 97
music, 106
folk, 106
opera, 106
Rustavi Choir, 110

national identity, 7, 19, 69
natural resources
clay, 51, 124, 125, 129
mineral ores, 50
nonferrous metals, 50, 135
oil, 51, 52, 130, 135

organizations
International Monetary Fund, 47
North Atlantic Treaty Organization, 33
United Nations, 35, 40, 41, 59
World Bank, 47

parliament, 19, 35, 38, 40, 43, 59, 141
Georgian Supreme Soviet, 35
people, 65
Adjarians, 64
Arabs, 23
Armenians, 67
Azerbaijanis, 67
Georgians, 62–63
Kartvelian, 62–64
Mingrelians, 63
Svans, 64
Ossetians, 66
plateau, 11
Iori Plateau, 11, 133
Kartalinian Plain, 11, 50, 133
poet, 13, 89, 103, 104, 115, 138
Galaktion Tabidze, 104
Lia Sturua, 104
Paolo Iashvili, 104
Shota Rustaveli, 13, 25, 63, 89, 102, 138
Titsian Tabidze, 104
political parties, 32, 39
Communist Party, 29, 30, 35, 39, 138
Georgian Social Democrats, 30
Green Party, 59
National Movement, 36, 39
Round Table, 32
Social Democratic Party, 29
pollution, 55, 57, 58, 59
air, 58–59
water, 57
ports, 53
Poti, 14, 28, 53, 133
Sukhumi, 14, 41, 52, 53, 87, 103, 109, 112, 133
president, 32, 33, 38, 43, 44, 139
Eduard Shevardnadze, 32, 33, 36, 44, 138, 139
Mikhail Saakashvili, 33, 36, 37, 39, 139
privatization, 48
public ownership, 48

recipes
chakhobili, 130
gozinake, 131
regions, 12
administrative regions, 12
religion
Christianity, 21, 24, 79, 80, 81, 83, 89, 97, 119, 136
Christians, 13, 40, 42, 66, 67, 83
Islam, 24, 43, 79, 84, 85
Muslims, 13, 25, 40, 45, 64, 65, 66, 67
Judaism, 24, 85
Vardzia Caves, 25, 100, 101
resort towns, 114–115
revolutions
Bolshevik Revolution, 30
Rose Revolution, 33, 36, 45, 139, 141
Russian Revolution, 29, 76, 94, 121
rivers, 10, 17, 52, 98
Enguri, 10
Kodori, 10, 41, 133
Kura River, 11, 13, 100, 133
Rioni, 10, 14, 17, 50, 52, 133
rulers
King Ashot I, 23
King Bagrat III, 23
King Bagrat IV, 23, 24
King David the Builder, 14, 98, 99, 138
King Giorgi II, 24
King Giorgi IV Lasha, 25
King Giorgi V, 25
King Vakhtang Gorgasali, 13, 21, 99, 115
Queen Tamar, 14, 25, 89, 98, 101, 102, 138

seas
Black Sea, 7, 10, 14, 15, 17, 19, 20, 25, 51, 53, 57, 58, 65, 83, 92, 114, 133
Caspian Sea, 11, 24, 51
South Ossetian Autonomous Region, 35, 42, 66
sports, 17, 111, 112, 113
climbing, 111
rugby, 113
skiing, 53, 111, 136
soccer, 112
Tskhenburti, 113
wrestling, 113
Stalin, Joseph, 28, 30, 31, 66, 80, 104, 107, 129

tourism, 47, 53, 141
trade, 9, 21, 23, 24, 27, 28, 45, 47, 135
traditional costume, 67
Transcaucasian Soviet Federated Republic, 30
transportation, 47, 48, 49, 51, 135
Georgian Military Highway, 9, 10, 52, 99, 111, 133
Klukhor Pass, 9, 133
Mamison Pass, 9, 133
rail, 52, 53
roads, 9–10, 15–16, 21–22, 52–53, 53, 71–72
subway, 13, 53
treaties
Peace of Amasia, 26
Treaty of Georgievsk, 27

unemployment rate, 69
Upper Svaneti, 9, 10, 50, 64, 101, 111, 133

village, 10, 47, 55, 74, 110, 117

wars
Civil war, 32
World War I, 29, 138
World War II, 30, 117, 120, 138
welfare, 77
workforce, 69
writers, 104
Akaki Tsereteli, 104
Ilya Chavchavadze, 104